ATLANTIS IN WISCONSIN

New Revelations About

Lost Sunken City

Frank Joseph

1998
Galde Press, Inc.
PO Box 460, Lakeville, MN 55044 U.S.A.

FIRST EDITION
Third Printing, 1998

Cover map courtesy of Minnesota Historical Society

Library of Congress Cataloging-in-Publication Data

Joseph, Frank.
 Atlantis in Wisconsin : new revelations about the lost sunken city
 / Frank Joseph.
  p. cm.
 Includes bibliographical references.
 ISBN 1–880090–12–0
 1. Megalithic monuments—Wisconsin—Rock Lake (Jefferson County)
 2. Atlantis. 3. Pyramids—Wisconsin—Rock Lake (Jefferson County)
 4. Rock Lake (Jefferson County, Wis.)—Antiquities.
 5. Parapsychology and archaeology. I. Title.
 E43.J65 1995
 977.5'85—dc20   94–45623
                                                          CIP

Galde Press, Inc.
PO Box 460
Lakeville, Minnesota 55044

About Frank Joseph

Frank Joseph is a feature writer and book reviewer for *Fate, Aviation Heritage, World War II* and various aviation and New Age publications in the U.S. and abroad. A scuba diver since his student days at Chicago's Mendel Catholic High School, he is a member of the Underwater Archaeological Society and has conducted dives in the Eastern Mediterranean, the Canary Islands off the coast of North Africa, at Yucatan and the Bahamas. Since 1980, he has devoted most of his research to investigating the lost civilization of Atlantis. He is also a member of the Oriental Institute at the University of Chicago, the Ancient Earthworks Society at the University of Wisconsin, Madison, and the Atlantis Organization at Buena Vista, Calif.

Other Books by Frank Joseph

The Destruction of Atlantis (Atlantis Research Publishers, Illinois, 1987)
Sacred Sites (Llewellyn Publications, St. Paul, Minnesota, 1992)
The Lost Pyramids of Rock Lake (Galde Press, St. Paul, Minnesota, 1992)

Forthcoming

The Last of the Red Devils
Echoes of Atlantis
The Survivors of Atlantis

Contents

Acknowledgements

I am indebted to Walter Krajewski for his invaluable assistance in the physical production of this book, and no less grateful to Wayne May for his collection of documents he so graciously put at my disposal. Special thanks, too, go to Dr. James Scherz, whose insights into the archaeological mysteries of his state helped to clarify some of the enigmas tackled in the following pages. Just as crucial to our discoveries was the unstinting labor and infectious enthusiasm of Lloyd Hornbostel.

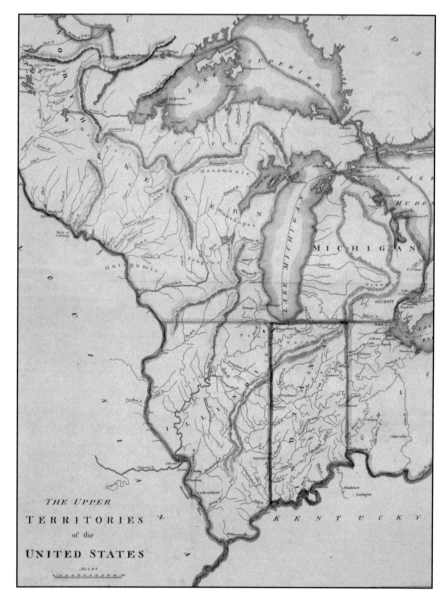

THE UPPER
TERRITORIES
of the
UNITED STATES

Map courtesy of the Minnesota Historical Society

Introduction

Magic on the Lake

I will arise and go now, for always night and day,
I hear lake water lapping with low sounds by the shore;
While I stand on the roadway, or on the pavements gray,
I hear it in the deep heart's core.

—William Butler Yeats

Alone figure carefully made his way across the silent ice cap that covered Tyranena. Brilliant bands of sharply defined twilight stratified the western horizon: azure, orange, yellow, gold, crimson. The sun had just vanished beneath the cloudless horizon. Overhead arched the great, blue-black dome of the heavens alight with stars. No sound, not a breath of wind disturbed the deep-winter chill, making the air seem rare and pure. It was as though the entire lake had been invisibly encased under glass.

This was a holy night, the cause for the man's solitary pilgrimage across the ice. On his back he bore long branches and a thin board. In his pack he carried apparently commonplace but magical items. He was a shaman, what some today might call a professional psychic. At the very center of the frozen lake, he put down his burden, then used an auger to drill three large holes through the ice in a triangular pattern. The sudden gush of black water frightened him as the auger broke through the thick ice cap. He was disturbing the Spirit Guardian, and he felt its terrifying power surging in the inky depths below. But he continued with his task.

Dusk sank deeper in the west, like a dying red ember, while the stars gazed down on him with growing intensity. His heart beat faster. He sensed the growing presence of ghostly entities. Quickly but deliberately, he laid the branches out on the solid face of the lake, one by one, end to end, from one hole to the next, delineating a triangle. Beginning at the north, he faced the four cardinal directions in turn to ask their blessing, and he prayed to the last light of day for protection and enlightenment. Then he stepped into the sacred triangle, at once aware of its distinct atmosphere, colder still than the winter that lay upon Tyranena. The world was dead calm as he knelt before the northernmost hole in the ice. Over it he spread the open palms of his hands in supplication and greeting. Then he put down the wooden board. Beside it he set up a small metal incense burner, in which he ignited fragrant leaves of sage. Nearby, he laid a personal crystal on the ice. Then, successively into each of the ice holes—north, east, south and west—he sprinkled pinches of tobacco, returning to kneel as before.

"Receive this token of my pure heart," he said aloud, then dropped his crystal into the black water. The sparkling mineral vanished just as thoroughly as if it had been swallowed up by the lake monster Spirit Guardian. While the thin blue-gray line of burning sage incense twisted like an insubstantial cord into the evening sky, the shaman prayed to the spirits of the holy men, chiefs, their wives and children, whose honored remains lay far down in the impenetrable water, under pyramidal piles of stone at the very bottom of the chasms and ravines that composed the lightless floor of Tyranena. He asked for their blessing on his people, who still groped in darkness.

"Know we venerate you! Grant us your enlightenment!" His hands went to the talking board. "I listen for your words, Holy Ones! If I am unwelcome, give me sign to leave. If I am worthy, tell me what I must do." He felt their presence gathering around him and, magically, the piece upon the board started to move ever so slightly. But it stopped before really beginning and remained mute, motionless. Thinking he had failed to win the spirits' trust, he nonetheless thanked them for hearing him. "My people and I shall always honor you." He dumped the still-burning sage sizzling into the water that was already starting to film over with fresh ice. The talking board, which had not talked this night, was packed away. He snapped the tamarack branches that had formed the triangle into smaller pieces, then stuffed them into the three holes to break down the sacred precinct and to prevent ghosts from following him home.

The shaman stood quietly for a prolonged moment, hearkening in the frigid, windless night under the heaven-high spray of stars. But he more sensed than heard someone—something—approaching him. A shadow out of the darkness was emerging across the silent face of the ice cap. He stood rooted in fear. Had the gods thought him blasphemous? Were they sending him some punishment in the form of an evil spirit? The figure came closer. It did not appear to be a man, and it was making straight for him. The night sky was bright with constellations; he could see the shadow clearly now. It spoke a greeting in a light tone and inquired what the shaman was doing.

"Good," he replied, "I am doing good." And he smiled in relief, because he knew the boy was sent from the gods, an omen unconscious of his own timely significance, whose portentous appearance the shaman would later attempt to interpret in all its mystical import with fellow adepts around a warm fire. The lad was the Sacred Androgyne, the living victory of opposing elements, the embodiment of harmony, balance—and that was good enough for the medicine man.

They separated, the boy to his family, the shaman to his council fire. His night's work had been received after all.

Psychic Archaeology at Rock Lake
The magic ritual just described took place at Rock Lake, a small body of water in southern Wisconsin between Milwaukee and Madison, not centuries ago, when the state was occupied solely by Winnebago and other native American tribes, but in the winter of 1989. It involved a modern-day shaman. It has been cited here to show that something about the lake and its nearby archaeological park, Aztalan, continues to draw those seeking access to the esoteric qualities peculiar to these associated sites.

A select group meets each spring and summer atop Aztalan's Pyramid of the Moon, an earthen temple-mound made by the ancient inhabitants of Wisconsin. Their ritual activity there, like that of many other persons almost instinctively drawn to the area, is part of its ongoing history. My purpose in this volume has been to investigate that "other side" of events surrounding the sacred sites—not at the expense of archaeology, but in combination with it.

Archaeology should be a multidisciplinary science if it is to become successful. Police departments around the world frequently employ successful psychics to assist them in the solution of serious crimes, particularly murders and disappearances. Often, these sensitive persons achieve spectacular results. If they consistently failed to come up with anything useful, they would not presently be in such universal demand by law enforcement agencies everywhere. Yet establishment archaeologists throw up their hands in horrified embarrassment at the mere mention of psychic assistance in matters of artifact identification or field work.

Especially impressive and most cogent to our investigation was the wholehearted acceptance of psychic abilities in the cause of science by J. Norman Emerson. Revered by his peers as "the father of Canadian archaeology," he was the principal archaeologist at the University of Toronto for thirty years, where he was acclaimed as the leading authority on the Huron and Iroquois. Founder and president of the Canadian Archaeological Association, acknowledged as one of the most important scientific bodies in the world. Dr. Emerson boldly announced before his colleagues in 1973, "It is my conviction that I have received knowledge without archaeological artifacts and archaeological sites from a psychic informant who relates this information to me without any evidence of the conscious use of reasoning. By means of the intuitive and parapsychological, a whole new vista of man and his past stands ready to be grasped. As an anthropologist and as an archaeologist trained in these fields, it makes sense to me to seize the opportunity to pursue and study the data thus provided. This should take first priority."

Through the use of a trusted psychic, Dr. Emerson was able to make several important finds, the most notable being the identity and time-placement of an ancient ceremonial pipe and the discovery of a structure inhabited by Samuel de Champlain in 1615, thus confirming the great French explorer's controversial (until then) visit to Quebec.[1]

Among the most remarkable examples of paranormal archaeology belonged to the twentieth century's foremost psychic, America's "Sleeping Prophet," Edgar Cayce. In 1943, he predicted, while under his usual trance state, that the first material evidence of Atlantean civilization would be found off the shores of Bimini, a tiny, obscure island in the Bahamas, in 1968. Cayce died two years after this prediction. In 1968, a private pilot flying over the northern shore of Bimini happened to see what appeared to be an immense "road" under the Caribbean. Investigators since its discovery have established that the structure represents the remains of a stone harbor formerly above sea level some 4,000 years ago. Many are convinced that the Bimini Wall is the first physical evidence for the lost civilization of Atlantis.

Notwithstanding the academics' outdated reactions, psychics have rendered valuable service to physical exploration of the past, most notably with California's Mobius Society, whose members made some remarkable finds in Egypt. At Alexandria, underwater archaeologists were led to the remains of a third-century-B.C. harbor. Today, Atlantis Organization investigators steer side-scan sonar sweeps off the shores of Bimini according to directions provided by onboard psychics. Impressed by these professional and exciting efforts and undeterred by the jeers of detractors, I was determined to make use of well-reputed psychics, just as I would call upon any other specialist whose expertise might contribute to our understanding of Wisconsin's prehistory. So far, our six-year-long investigation had attracted scuba divers, aviators, photographers, hydrologists, surveyors, anthropologists, and archaeologists. There was still room for a psychic or two.

But I did not surrender to the paranormal, either. I was intent on maintaining a balance of forces in which the psychic figured proportionately among the other field experts. Hence this book offers a mix of standard investigation and psychic research. The conclusions at which both arrived independently of each other were surprisingly complementary. Far from mutually excluding one another, our psychometric readings and the latest archaeological information often paralleled and converged. Usually, the psychic impressions clarified and made convincingly logical those points only suggested or partially explained by the physical evidence. There was never any conflict between psychic analysis and "pure science." Even so, I have seen fit not to merge the two, but to compartmentalize them for clarity's sake. Together, but distinct, both methods provide, I hope, a broader panorama in which to examine the dramatic sweep of the Rock Lake/Aztalan phenomenon, which, in any case, cannot be satisfactorily explained by the standard scientific method alone.

Indeed, the revelations of our modern-day seers seemed to make the long-dead actors of those ancient events come alive. They shook off the dust of dispassionate study and assumed a sense of flesh-and-blood identity that at once restored part of their humanity, while touching a resonant chord of empathy in ourselves. A case in point was Marene Martensen's description of the Beaded Princess. While a psychic reading may only find fleeting correspondence in the cold, archaeological record, Marene's account of this magical personality who lived a thousand years ago has that ring of credibility which is the hallmark of truth. At the very least, she has given us a plausible verbal diorama of life as it might have been in ancient Aztalan.

It is, after all, by way of our imaginative faculty that the hazy past may be brought into present focus. The psychic insights of Marene and her colleagues flesh out that indistinct middle ground beyond the limits of scientific investigation, between physical evidence and human events. Those moments when the two apparently contrary methods cross-reference each other—confirm and validate each other's findings from different points of view—are thrilling, because they telescope our vision far into the prehistoric drama of our country. And it is a high drama scarcely suspected by most Americans.

The Story of Aztalan

But what is—or was—Aztalan? And what is its relationship to Rock Lake, with its alleged sunken pyramids, only three miles away? Well, it's a long story—about twelve thousand years long, and bizarre enough in the bare telling without paranormal additions.

As the last glaciers retreated northward across Wisconsin, they carved out a very small lake, hardly more than a deep, elongated pond, in what is now Jefferson County. Over the next nine centuries, small bands of primitive human hunters sometimes labeled by anthropologists as "Archaeo-Indians" filtered across the southern part of the state.

But around 3000 B.C., the little lake area was suddenly transformed by the arrival of large numbers of foreigners from across the sea. They sailed down from Michigan's Upper Peninsula, where they mined colossal quantities of raw copper and settled, some of them, around the lake shore. They buried their honored dead under great stone monuments—cone-shaped pyramids, volcano-like sepulchers, and tent-shaped crypts. The memorials grew in number over the years to form a necropolis, or city of the dead, called Tirajana, after the name of a royal family of seafaring miners. Tirajana became their focal point for the copper trade, through which it prospered for eighteen centuries.

Then, about 1200 B.C., that trade collapsed, and Tirajana, under the pressures of native hostility, was abandoned. But not before its inhabitants, seeking to protect the graves of their ancestors from desecration, opened a canal from a nearby river on higher ground. A massive flood deluged the lake, drowning its necropolis under an additional fifty feet of water and expanding its shores to more than two miles across. The civilizers fled, some to the distant, southern lands of the Mayas, where they intermarried with the native aristocracy.

In the ensuing centuries, Tirajana became Tyranena in the speech of the local Plains Indians, who continued to revere the lake with its sunken monuments as a sacred center. Around A.D. 900, the Maya leadership of Yucatan's mixed descendants left with their followers for the Gulf of Mexico. They worshiped time, which they perceived as the omnipotent god of the universe, and, seeking to live according to his calendar, the Mayas migrated up the Mississippi, there dedicating to him a great city in south-central Illinois.

The Birth of Aztalan
Referred to now as Cahokia, the pyramidal ceremonial center grew over the next two hundred years to include more than thirty thousand residents. In A.D. 1100, their sacred calendar told them to move on again, so they abandoned Cahokia and wandered into southern Wisconsin, on to Tyranena. Honoring its underwater city of the dead, they extended its necropolis to include the shoreline, where they raised the gigantic effigy mound of a serpent, the image of a spirit guardian they conjured into the lake.

East of Tyranena, they built a scaled-down version of Cahokia, a twenty-one-acre city of three pyramids surrounded by stockaded walls in triplicate and covered with white plaster. The masters of this complex enclosure were astronomer-priests, whose observations of the sky won them great influence. People came to them from enormous distances for information about planting, harvesting, sailing, and religious ceremonies of all kinds, bartering food and luxury goods for the wisdom of the heavens. Knowledge was power, and the walled city extended its political sway over southern Wisconsin and northern Illinois. The civilizers rechristened the necropolis lake as Chicomoztoc, or the Womb, because that name epitomized their religion of eternal rebirth, which was celebrated in nighttime rituals at the shore. They referred to their city as Aztalan, or Water Town, for its location on the banks of the Crawfish River.

But after the beginning of the fourteenth century, a major social crisis was brewing behind the great enclosure, while the sacred calendar wound down to the end of another critical epoch. Around A.D. 1320, the inhabitants of Aztalan set fire to their own capital. Flames engulfed its high walls and everything they contained, as the Aztalaners evacuated Wisconsin toward the south. They migrated as far as the Valley of Mexico, where they recreated their forsaken Chicomoztoc in a new city, Tenochitlan, which became the capital of the Aztec state.

When, in the early nineteenth century, modern European immigrants arrived at the shores of the small Wisconsin lake, still known to the local Winnebago Indians as Tyranena, they were unaware of its dramatic past, save for native myths of the "rock tepees" beneath its surface. In response to this legend, the newcomers renamed it Rock Lake. Even this oral tradition was eventually forgotten, until 1900, when the sunken structures were glimpsed by two fishermen during a drought. Efforts to relocate, identify, and study the drowned necropolis continued with varying success through the twentieth century, culminating in a sonar sweep of the lake bottom in 1989. Since then, the pyramidal objects have been found and photographed, but controversy still surrounds their real origin.

That, in a nutshell, is the strange tale of the lost pyramids of Rock Lake, according to the best evidence I have been able to assemble in six years of investigation. But it is not the end of the story. Who were the ancient civilizers, the prehistoric seamen and builders of the stone pyramids? Where did they come from and what became of the half billion pounds of copper they mined from the Upper Great Lakes Region? What was it like to live in prehistoric America? This present volume tries to answer those questions and addresses its research to many more mysteries about ancient America. The human events that took place behind the walls of Aztalan or what is now the bottom of Rock Lake are not lost historical curiosities, but vital keys to unlocking the precious secrets of our country's deep and unsuspected past.

•1•

The Elder's Tale

In the earthquake of ancient peoples new springs break forth.
—Friedrich Nietzsche
Thus Spake Zarathustra

I must die," the old man said without regret. "It will be a good thing. I am tired of carrying around this old body of flesh and bones like a sack of dried leaves and kindling at the end of autumn. Throw them into the fire to keep the young ones warm!" He laughed sincerely. His face was a map of wrinkled leather, but a single, deeply sunken eye barely glistened from behind its heavily folded eyelid like the glint of a dagger's blade through a worn-out buckskin sheath.

"I have the freedom of an old man about to die. If I go with my secrets, I might have to come back as a crow. You will not understand any of my cawing, no matter how hard I try to tell you. It will be too late then. Besides, I see the time coming when you white men must learn from us, else my people, your people, everyone—ssshhh!" And he made an apocalyptic gesture with his strong, gnarled hand. It looked as though it had grown naturally from the bough of some antediluvian oak.

We were gathered in the elder's tent, somewhere in northern Wisconsin, near the shores of Lake Superior. I cannot divulge his name, nor even mention the identity of his tribe. All I may relate is a paraphrase of some of the things he shared with us one winter, not long ago. We were quietly attentive, as his eyes, still fiercely eagle-like for all their eighty-odd years, gazed beyond our time into the little fire around which we sat. He spoke not a word for long moments in the expectant silence, then suddenly but deliberately defined a broad circle in the near darkness with both hands before beginning in a voice younger and louder than before.

"When the stars which men see in the night sky were not in the same places they are now, our fathers had already fished these waters for many turns. They were like children, no wiser than deer, but happy. The red metal on the ground and in streams they found and made into ornaments for their hair and hands. That was all it meant to them. But over the Sunrise Sea, in a big lodge on a great island, the Marine Men prayed to Wes-a-hee-sa, the Foolish Creator. 'Give us the red metal!' they cried to him. 'In it there is much Manitou for us!' Their shamans were clever, their magic was strong. Wes-a-hee-sa turned his ear to them. He told them how to make big canoes and he led them across the waves from the Old Red Land, the island of the great lodge, to Turtle Island. They came to where now we sit.

Evil From the Sea
"Our fathers, when they saw the strangers, ran away. They thought they were gods or evil spirits. Their hair was like fire, their eyes like ice, their skin had no color. For their clothes were made from the rainbow, but the men among them had faces like bears. Only few of their women came with them. They carried a magic stone. When they threw it on the ground, it sang a song telling them where to dig holes in the Earth Mother's breast. It was an evil thing to wound the Mother of us all. But, in time, even some of our fathers joined the Marine Men. They stole the red metal and put it in their big canoes.

Down the rivers they went, into the south. The waters were greater then than they are today. The Earth Mother, in her distress and anger, shrank them to prevent the foreign chiefs from returning. But in those days their big canoes could go anywhere. They went to a small lake, Tyranena. It was named after one of their chiefs from the Old Red Land. They made the lake shore a sacred burial ground and worshiped the moon as a powerful, divine woman. They performed evil magic with the red metal at this place. Then they put it back into the big canoes, which took it away to their great lodge over the Sunrise Sea.

"The Marine Men buried their dead in pits. When they were laid inside, side by side, in great numbers, stones were gathered, then stacked up over the graves in a big mound. Smaller mounds, like rock tepees, they piled up over chiefs and their families. The mounds and stone tepees they covered in white and painted many magic signs on them to imitate the dances of the stars. The dead were supposed to learn these dances, if they wanted to go to the place of the Great Spirit. Sun and moon exchanged places many times and the burial grounds grew to become a big town of dead people. Our fathers performed much heavy work for the Marine Men at this place. But one day the Earth Mother could bear her torment no longer and she pulled the Old Red Land under the water. The great lodge with many Marine Men drowned. Then those who were over here were afraid. They fled from the many holes they made to find the red metal. But our fathers, seeing their chance, attacked them, killing many. The sinful foreign chiefs ran to Tyranena and the big mounds of their dead tribesmen, calling to their spirits for protection from the wrath of the Attiwandeton and the Chippewa.

"One of their shamans spoke. 'The dead will not save us,' he said, 'unless we save *them*. They command you to preserve their graves from harm, or else they will become ghosts and have to roam the world forever.' 'How can we protect them, when we cannot even protect ourselves?,' they cried. 'You must dig a long row from the river to the lake!' This they did. And when it was done, the shaman opened a door from the ditch, which was higher than the lake. When he did this, the river ran faster and louder than a buffalo herd. A mighty waterfall of many thunders fell on Tyranena. The great flood rushed over the mounds and rock tepees with their honored dead. They were buried under the wall of waters.

After the Flood

"When the flood was complete, the shaman used his magic to conjure a great beast that would live forever in the lake to guard the graves from desecration. This task done, the last of the Marine Men fled Tyranena. As promised by the spirits of their ancestors, they were protected from further harm. Some built big canoes and went back over the Sunrise Sea, notwithstanding the destruction of the Old Red Land.

"Others went south, into the hot lands of valleys and mountains and jungles. They lived long with the people there. They became chiefs again and had sons by the native women. Their sons begat more sons and on through many generations, until one day the sun god told them to return to Tyranena.

"They honored the sacred lake by causing the figures of its spirit guardian to be made on the shore. Tyranena they now called the Lake of the Seven Caves, after the seven tribes which came up from the south. They used its shores for the burial of their dead under mounds of holy soil. Then they went to the river, where they built a great wall. They lived behind it and grew rich because all the people brought them food and hides. In exchange, they gave the Indians words from the sky gods, who told them how to regulate their lives and their crops. All went well for some generations. They even robbed the Earth Mother again of her red metal. They gave it to their people in the hot lands of the south. They called their place of the big walls, Aztalan. Our fathers did not know what this name meant, so they just called it the Old City.

The Fall of Aztalan
"One day, the young chief of Aztalan took a bride from the people who lived outside the walls. According to their law, this was a bad thing to do. But the man's passion prevailed and she came to live in the Old City with her family. Her brothers worshiped demons and honored them by eating human flesh. They won some of the Aztalaners over to these death gods. There was much confusion. Then the sun god came again. He was very angry and told the people they had to leave the Old City. He blew hot winds, dried up all the water, and kept the corn from ripening as punishment. To purify the sacred ground they had desecrated, the Aztalaners burned the walls and set fire to everything. Then they left, going back into the valley lands of the far south. I heard they became a great people again, until white men came and killed them all.

"Now, this is the story we and other tribal elders know. It was given to us by our grandfathers from their grandfathers. We preserve it as a lesson for our people. These Marine Men and their sons insulted the gods with their profane greed. Each time they suffered. Many died. They lost all they sought for. The time is coming again. Earth Mother and Sky Father warn us to become good children. They threaten us with the great punishment. It has happened before. It will happen again. That is the lesson of Tyranena and Aztalan."

•2•

Missing—Half a Billion
Pounds of Copper

Effodiuntur opes, irritatementa malorum. (Riches, the incentives to evil, are dug out of the earth.)

—*Ovid*

In *The Lost Pyramids of Rock Lake*, I included a chapter entitled "The Great Copper Mystery." Space limitations at that time prevented me from reproducing most of the information I had accumulated about this intriguing enigma, so only brief excerpts of my complete research could be presented. But in order to properly describe the underlying powers responsible for events in ancient Wisconsin, a full explanation of the mysterious copper question needed to be made. The present volume affords an opportunity to present this question in its entirety and uncut, as perhaps the most revealing insight into the lost history of prehistoric America.

Beginning around 3000 B.C., in excess of five hundred thousand tons of copper were mined in Michigan's Upper Peninsula, with most activity taking place at Isle Royale, an island in Lake Superior at the Canadian border. This half-a-billion-pound estimate is a *conservative* figure; the actual tonnage was certainly much greater, possibly twice as large. The mines abruptly and inexplicably shut down in 1200 B.C., reopening no less mysteriously twenty-three hundred years later. From then until A.D. 1320, some additional two thousand tons were

5

removed, destination unknown. As before, operations were suddenly suspended for no apparent cause. Tools—mauls, picks, hammers, shovels, and levers—were left by their unknown owners in place. Octave DuTemple, a foremost authority on early Michigan, asks, "Why did these miners leave their operations and implements as though planning on taking up their labors the next day, and yet mysteriously never returned?"[1]

William P.F. Ferguson writes, "The work is of a colossal nature," and "amounted to the turning over of the whole formation to their depth and moving many cubic acres (it would not be seriously extravagant to say cubic miles) of rock."[2]

The prehistoric mines were no crude holes in the ground, but incredibly effective operations to extract staggering masses of raw material as quickly as possible. An average of one thousand to twelve hundred tons of ore were excavated per pit, yielding about a hundred thousand pounds of copper each.[3] To achieve such prodigious yields, the mysterious miners employed simple techniques that enabled them to work with speed and efficiency. They created intense fires atop a copper-bearing vein, heated the rock to very high temperatures, then doused it with water. The rock fractured and stone tools were employed to extract the copper. Deep in the pits, a vinegar mixture was used to speed spalling (breaking of the rock in layers) and reduce smoke. How such high temperatures were applied is part of the enigma. The bottom of a fire sitting on a rock face is its coolest part. Even especially hot cane fires would take a long time to sufficiently heat the vein for spalling, if at all. How the prehistoric miners directed concentrated, acetylene temperatures to the ground is a disturbing question modern technology is unable to answer.

The Magnitude of the Mining
The ancient enterprise was a truly mind-boggling affair, including about five thousand mines, mostly along the Keweenaw Peninsula and the eastern end of Lake Superior above St. Mary's River. On the northern shore, the diggings extended 150 miles, varying in width from four to seven miles, through the Trap Range, to include three Michigan counties (Keweenaw, Houghton, and Ontonagon). At Isle Royale, the mining area was forty miles long and averaged five miles across. The pits ran practically in a contiguous line for thirty miles through the Rockland region, as they did at greater intervals in the Ontonagon District. If all these pits were placed end to end, single file,

they would form a manmade trench more than five miles long, twenty feet wide and thirty feet deep.[4]

The genius of these third-millennium-B.C. miners extended to their unknown but highly accurate methods for locating copper veins. Every historic Lake Superior mine opened over the last two hundred years was previously worked by the Ancients, who mined all the productive veins throughout the region. DuTemple writes, "As some of these veins did not out-crop at the surface, but were discovered only upon excavation, it is seen that these prehistoric peoples possessed a gift or ability which present day man would find very valuable."[5] Jacob Houghton argues that all the veins had been recently exposed by glacial action and were therefore easily discernible to the ancient prospectors, who needed no extraordinary "gift" or "ability" to find the copper.[6]

H.H. Winchell, too, believed they simply followed along an observable copper-bearing belt of rock laid bare by freshly retreating glaciers.[7] Houghton nevertheless admits that, "The ancient miners made few mistakes in the selection of deposits to be wrought. In almost every instance in the places where they had carried on extensive mine work, they have been wrought in successful mines of these later days."[8] But more recent understanding about Upper Peninsula geology confirms that the whole region, as it appears today, was essentially unchanged for five thousand years before the first copper mines were opened, so the glaciers did not expose the copper veins for the prehistoric prospectors, after all.[9]

Who Were the Ancient Miners?
The Menomonie Indians of northern Wisconsin preserve a tribal memory about the ancient copper miners, described as a light-skinned "foreign people," who discovered ore-bearing veins by throwing magical stones, called Yuwipi, on the ground, which made the copper-rich rocks "ring, as brass does."[10] Remarkably, the Menomonie legend appears to conform to or at least suggest a prospecting technique actually practiced by European miners more than three thousand years ago. Bronze with a high tin content (from one part in four to one in six or seven) emits a full, resonant sound when struck with a stone. Such bronze is today known as "bell metal" for the ringing tone it produces.[11] To the ancestors of the Menomonie, the native copper and manufactured bronze, of which they knew nothing, must have seemed one and the same. When they saw the bronze being struck with a stone to test its quality by the

chime-sound it made, they assumed the copper had been magically transformed by the Yuwipi. In any case, the bell-metal quality of bronze strongly implies that native accounts of ancient copper mining in the Upper Great Lakes were undertaken there by a non-Amerindian people. S.A. Barrett, the first professional archaeologist at Aztalan, had to admit, "Now, unless there is some mistake as to these facts, we are not disposed to attribute this work (the copper mines) to the aboriginal inhabitants. The keepers, levers, wooden bowls, etc., are rather indicative of Caucasian ingenuity and art."[12]

By way of comparison with the prehistoric achievement in Michigan, the first modern mine at Isle Royale was inaugurated in 1771 by British engineers, who failed to extract enough minerals to make their enterprise worthwhile before it had to be shut down. It was not until seventy years later that the copper sources, all of them known and worked by the Ancients five thousand years before, were found. Their prehistoric mines only came to light in 1847. The Calumet and Hecla Conglomerate, employing modern technology and electric power, removed 509 million tons of copper between 1929 and 1949, compared to the same tonnage mined by an unknown people during the heyday of the Egyptian pharaohs.[13]

As Roy W. Drier writes, "There is not a mine operating today in the district that has not had its prehistoric workings. This fact was so well established in the early days [of modern mining] that the evidence of ancient work was sought as a guide to present loads. The development of the Calumet was certainly hastened by the finding of the old mound, and many of the other mines owe votes of thanks to these mysterious, unknown, prehistoric workers."[14]

Nor did they dig up only small fragments. Masses of copper rock six thousand pounds and more were excavated and raised on well-made cribwork, stone and timber platforms used to lift ponderous material to the surface. These cribs were usually made of shaped boughs organized to resemble a log cabin that could be raised by a series of levers and wedges.[15] An example of the massive portions mined in ancient Michigan was the so-called Ontonagon Boulder. Removed to the Smithsonian Institution around the turn of the century, it weighs no less than five tons. A six-ton copper mass was discovered *in situ* on one of the raised cribs, where it appears to have been abandoned on the day the miners suddenly quit the pits. Partially trimmed of its spurs and projecting points, it was ten feet long, three feet wide, and two feet thick.[16]

Estimates of 10,000 men working the mines for a thousand years seem credible, as does the conclusion that they were not slaves, because the miners carried away their dead.[17] No ancient graves nor evidence of cremations have been found in the Upper Peninsula. Indeed, virtually all they left behind were their tools, literally millions of them. As far back as 1840, ten wagonloads of stone hammers were taken from a single location near Rockland. Those in McCargo Cove, on the north side of Isle Royale, amounted to a thousand tons.[18] The mauls were mass produced in various sizes and types to serve different tasks. Some were only 2.4-pound hand-held tools for finishing and shaping. Others weighed forty pounds and more. Fastened to cables suspended from a crossbar, they were swung like pendulums to batter the rock face and crush chunks of ore. Most hammers were five to ten pounds, grooved to fit a wooden handle tied around the middle. Generally egg-shaped, they were made of diabase, a hard, tough, fine-grained igneous rock.

Nor were these hammers crudely manufactured, despite their numbers. As Drier writes, "In examining the tools that have been recovered, one is involuntarily amazed at the perfection of workmanship and at their identity of form with the tools made for like purposes and used at the present day, the prototypes of the implements of our present civilization. The sockets of the spears, chisels, arrow-heads, knives and fleshers are, in nearly all instances, formed as symmetrically and perfectly as could be done by the best smith of the present day, with all the improved aids of his art."[19]

In addition to the superabundant mauls, many other kinds of well-crafted tools have been recovered from the ancient mines, such as graceful wood shovels strangely resembling oars, copper gads or wedges and chisels. The mines themselves were not simple pits, but outfitted with modernistic irrigation techniques to flush out debris and fill via substantial trenches, sometimes as long as 500 feet.[20] Wooden buckets and bailers of various sizes were common discoveries. The rich evidence of this huge mining enterprise bespeaks a "foreign tribe," as the Menomonie said, whose cultural sophistication shared nothing in common with America's archaeo-aboriginal populations.

Greatness on a Colossal Scale
But not a single human bone, pottery shard, nor artifact related to the prehistoric miners has been found in the copper region. In 1922, however, William A. Ferguson discovered the remains of a middle-sized

settlement on the north side of Isle Royale. Comprising only rectangular, shallow pits, it fronted an ancient boat-landing. As the discoverer
wrote, "it is interesting to note that the left bank of the Sibley, just
below the fall, where the land is only slightly above the water, appears
to have been protected by an embankment or levee, three or four feet
in height and running for something more than a half-mile."[21] The
great size of this landing suggests a harbor or docking facility ("I am
convinced of the artificial character of the embankment," says Ferguson), and it may have been the chief disembarkation point of the
island for freighters, a conclusion underscored by the close proximity
of the settlement.

It is the existence of this harbor which more than implies the use of
large sailing vessels by the ancient miners. A half-mile long levee
would not be required to land the birch-bark canoes used by Indians
of the Upper Great Lakes. Nor would these same canoes be able to
transport thousands of tons of raw copper across fifty miles of storm-
tossed Lake Superior from Isle Royale to the mainland. Indeed, the
waters there are still regarded as treacherous for modern ships and
would have been yet more perilous, even for large rafts, in earlier
times. Clearly, only a seafaring people with a tradition of advanced
shipbuilding and navigation skills could have regularly negotiated the
run from Isle Royale laden with heavy cargoes of copper.

No native Americans were proficient in such seamanship. Their
birch-bark canoes and wooden dugouts were superbly fitted for
rivers, streams, and lake coastal areas, but not for open water. They
could not have transported even the thousands of pounds of stone
diabase hammers from their supply source on the Canadian shore,
seventy-five miles away.

Outside the landing area, the Sibley site may have represented a
shelter of some kind for the miners, more likely a storage center. No
artifacts of any kind were found at the Sibley Stream dig, which reaf-
firmed that the ancient miners limited their operations to the brief,
warm-weather months, returning to their homes somewhere south of
the hard-frost line. As Charles Whittlesy asks, "May we not reasonably suppose that the miners came from the south and worked during
the summer months, returning to their homes in autumn? There is
nothing to show that the country was permanently inhabited by the
ancient miners and, as their works were open cuts and not galleries,
it must have been almost, if not quite, impracticable to work them in
winters of that latitude. No human graves have been found here that

can be referred to the era of the copper workings. Neither is there any evidence that there were furnaces or places where copper was refined or melted or where it was crushed in the rock and afterwards separated by washing, as we do now. It seems most probable that the people did not reside in the country, but came in the summer from a milder climate, bringing their provisions with them and taking away, on their return in the fall, the metal they had raised."[22]

W.H. Holmes writes succinctly, "It is unlikely, however, that any considerable amount of the shaping work was conducted on the island [Isle Royale]. It seems to me more likely that the pieces of metal obtained were carried away to distant centers of population to be worked by skilled artisans and we may justly assume that a considerable trade existed in the raw material."[23] Those "distant centers of population" were Rock Lake and Aztalan, which were connected to the Great Lakes mining areas by a belt of similar mounds. One Upper Peninsula temple-mound was ten feet tall, fifteen feet long, and virtually identical to Aztalan's Pyramid of the Moon. As we shall see, the ancient copper miners and the inhabitants of Rock Lake/Aztalan were one and the same people.

Ghosts of the "Marine Men"
Among the Menomonie, who continue to inhabit the Upper Peninsula after unguessed generations, references to ancient copper mining and Isle Royale are scant, but revealing. Still largely a forested wilderness of 230 square miles, fifty miles long and nine miles across, the island lies northwest of the Michigan shore and was the most intensely mined of all areas in the Great Lakes. It was here, too, that the largest copper deposits were excavated. Yet the Menomonie have little to say about this place. Their name for Isle Royale is Minong, or "Island of the Spirit," implying death.

Minong was, in fact, taboo, because a legend told how a party of Indians who once went ashore there were all, save one, killed by the Memogovissioois, or the ghosts of the "Marine Men," who long ago owned the island. The Menomonie still divert the prows of their canoes and even avert their gaze from its direction.[24] Minong is additionally protected by a monstrous spirit guardian, Michibissy, the ferocious water serpent, whose legend extended to Rock Lake, all of which demonstrates the natives wanted nothing to do with the island. The historic Menomonie are not synonymous with the ancient copper miners, despite their close proximity to the prehistoric pits. In fact, the resident Indians neither knew nor cared that the miners, known only to them as the seafaring "Marine Men," even existed, outside of a single reference to the magic Yuwipi stones, which a white-skinned "foreign people" used to find copper.

Among the Attiwandeton, formerly of the Great Lakes, was a tradition that recalled how their ancestors decimated a "white people" and seized both their lands and animals.[25] The Attiwandeton were, it is true, infamous for their depredations against the Iroquois and Huron in the mid-1600s. Coincidentally, the Chippewa know an identical account of a white-skinned tribe annihilated in the deep past. When shown a copper axe excavated from a mound in the late eighteenth century, Chippewa elders responded, "White man make long ago, way back."[26]

Father Claude Allouez, who traveled among the Chippewa in 1660, reported that they "esteem them (copper trinkets) as divinities or as presents given them to promote their happiness by the gods that dwell beneath the water. For this reason they preserve these pieces of copper wrapped up with their most precious articles." Some families, he observed, owned the copper items "time out of mind, being cherished as domestic gods."[27]

DuTemple writes, "Indian legends make no mention of these mining operations which were of a magnificence and a magnitude worthy of being included in the history of any race. The legends do mention that a white race was driven out far back in the Indians' history. The fact that Indian legends indicate that pieces of copper were revered as Manitous or gods would seem to prove that they were not the people who mined and used the copper industrially."[28]

The Copper Statue
While traveling through the Lake Superior territories, Father Allouez saw a one-foot tall statue sculpted entirely from a single, over-sized copper nugget and representing a man "with a beard like a European." It was the focus of idol-worship by the beardless Indians of the Outaouac country and appears to have been fashioned in the image of the white-skinned Marine Men who mined Michigan's copper, five thousand years ago.[29]

Despite their reverence for fragments of copper, native Americans never mined it, but picked up pieces of "float copper" deposited on the ground by retreating glaciers. They made only slight use of the shiny metal for baubles and a few tools, but that was all. As Jack

Parker wonders, "Why is there no link between the ancient miners and the present Indians?"[30]

Dr. James Fisher answered, "The civilization of this people (the miners) was of a much higher order than that of the succeeding races generally referred to as the North American Indians."[31] Houghton mentions, too, that skulls found in the mounds of Wisconsin are ortho-cephalic, occupying "a position between the Indian cranium, which is brachycephalic, and the Teutonic, which is dolicocephalic."[32] In other words, the Mound Builders, who appear at least related to the ancient copper miners, were a race apart from the native American tribal peoples and, based on comparative cranial analysis, would seem to have been the mixed offspring of the aboriginal population and Europoid visitors in prehistoric times.

America's ancient copper mines represent the key to unlocking Rock Lake's deepest secrets. The grandiose mining enterprise began suddenly around 3000 B.C. and terminated just as abruptly 1,800 years later. Investigators believe the mines were functioning at their peak capacity during the last century of operations, the same period when Rock Lake's pyramids adorned its early shoreline.

As late as the end of the nineteenth century, an undetermined number of conical stone pyramids and even linear mounds extended from the Upper Peninsula copper mines across the land to Rock Lake, which had its own, identical structures. Few survived the needs of the pioneers, who dismantled the pyramids to build wells, cattle cor-rals, and pig pens. The only existing examples were accidentally found as recently as 1987, in Oakland County, Michigan. Like Rock Lake's underwater monuments, the Oakland County features were almost perfectly circular, with a perimeter of larger stones.

As Betty Sodders quotes their discoverers, "it is obvious that each stone was carefully placed and fitted into a pile. The smaller stones inside the larger rocks were carefully sorted and selected, not just randomly dumped unceremoniously by some farmer anxious to clear his fields."[33] These Michigan structures so closely resemble some of the stone ruins observed on the bottom of Rock Lake, that it is obvious that both sites were expressions of the same culture.

In 1746, a French Jesuit, de Verandrier, "found enormous masses of stone placed in an up-right position by the hand of man, and on one of them was something which had been taken to be a Tartar inscrip-tion. It was engraved on a small tablet and which had been set into a pillar of cut stone, in which position it was found. Some of the Jesuits

assured Kalm (an interested explorer) that they had seen and handled the inscription. It was afterwards transmitted to Count Mau-
repas, in France."[34] Tragically, the "Tartar" inscription was lost
through too much handling, and even the great Alexander von Hum-
bolt's efforts to track it down proved in vain. Its loss was typical of the
wholesale disappearance of ancient American artifacts that continues
to this day. Knowledge of our country's deepest past has consequently
been cut off from investigators trying to piece together a badly frag-
mented prehistory.

Links to Rock Lake
But de Vrandrier's "enormous masses of stone placed in an up-right
position by the hand of man" were undoubtedly the same kind of
pyramidal structures identically encountered by divers under Tyranena, defining a line of cultural continuity stretching from the lake to
Michigan's ancient copper mines. It is intriguing to imagine that at
least one of the underwater pyramids might have its own "Tartar
inscription," a find that would blow the lid off American archaeology.

This cultural continuity linking southern Wisconsin to the Upper
Great Lakes was additionally reinforced in its Rock Lake identity by
Michigan's ridge-top mounds made of fitted stones, similar to the
subsurface Limnatis pyramid, a gigantic linear mound sixty feet below
the surface in the north-central quadrant. They were known to exist in
Michigan's Romeo and McComb Counties until the close of the last
century, when they were referred to by locals as "rock haycocks."
Although just five feet high, they stood only little more than a mile
from a set of earthworks not unlike those behind the walls of Aztalan.

Excavations of one of the "rock haycocks" revealed extended
human skeletons, recalling Wisconsin's Pyramid of the Moon, with its
ten full-length burials. Six miles from Michigan's Black River is an
enclosure surrounding numerous, conical mounds, mostly five feet tall
and all constructed of undressed river stones (at least one of the ridge-
top mounds at the bottom of Rock Lake was made of river stones) fitted together and bonded by a cement-like coating of mixed lime, the
same substance taken from subsurface structures in Rock Lake.

These Upper Peninsula pyramidal mounds of rough stone run in
a straight line from Michigan's prehistoric copper mining district to
Rock Lake/Aztalan. They establish an identifiable connection linking
the two areas and, in so doing, explain both their function and the reason for their once formidable numbers. The mining season in the

Great Lakes region was strictly circumscribed by brutal and sudden weather conditions. The ancient miners had only three months to extract the tons of copper they desired so passionately. Too early an arrival or too long a stay would not spell hardship alone, but death. Negotiating the treacherous waters around Isle Royale outside the mid-summer sailing season in vessels heavily laden with cargoes of raw copper would have been very risky.

The miners' cone-shaped pyramids that formerly dotted the landscape from northern Michigan into Rock Lake were timekeepers, sundials, and star-pointers upon whose sharply cast shadows and celestial alignments the ancient inhabitants kept a wary eye. As soon as the structures indicated the onset of fall, the miners shut down their mining season and cleared out of the Upper Peninsula. Their short digging period explains the obvious haste of their operations. They had to get as much copper out as quickly as possible, then head south from the imminent bad weather. Appropriately, Rock Lake/Aztalan lies just below the hard-snow line. Only fifty miles north, the winters are remarkably more severe.

Rock Lake was an ancient mining center, a clearing-house where raw copper extracted from the Great Lakes region was readied for shipment elsewhere and a home for the miners until they could return to Michigan the following summer. Precisely regulating all the stages of procedure in those widespread operations involved thousands of miners, handlers, sailors, overseers and workers of all kinds, together with an efficient calendrical technology that was vital to success and survival. Hence the abundance of astronomically significant structures stretching from Rock Lake to the Upper Peninsula. When prehistoric America's copper mining ceased all at once in 1200 B.C., the Michigan pits were abandoned for the next twenty-one centuries. They were suddenly reopened in A.D. 900, an event which can only mean that, despite the virtual abandonment of the Rock Lake area for thousands of years, it was continuously held in profound awe by numerous, successive generations among whose mythology the lake had achieved a powerfully sacred status that continues to this day in the oral traditions of such widespread tribes as the Menomonie and the Sioux.

From Michigan to Peru
The date for reopening Michigan's mines is enormously significant, because it coincides with the establishment of Cahokia, the greatest city in ancient North America above the Rio Grande. The overlords of

Cahokia were as interested in copper as their fourteenth century B.C. descendants in Wisconsin. Their pyramidal burials in south-central Illinois' prehistoric megalopolis are rich in copper armor and ornaments. But personal wealth accounted for only a small fraction of the tons of the imported mineral. Alliance with another mound-building people at Spiro, Oklahoma, near the Arkansas River, provided portage to Mesoamerica's trade centers. The Spiro seamen operated three-masted, thirty-foot long wooden hull vessels plying the Gulf of Mexico to Florida and Vera Cruz.

Cahokia, like older Rock Lake (Tyranena), had its astronomers, whose Woodhenge, a precisely arranged circle of twenty-foot-tall, red-painted cedar posts, calculated the positions of the sun. Thus provided with accurate celestial information, they knew when to dispatch their mining expeditions to the Upper Peninsula. Doubtless the site chosen for the foundation of Cahokia had been determined by its central location at the hub of trade routes converging from all over the continent.

When Cahokian society collapsed in A.D. 1100, much of its culture-bearing population migrated naturally to the Rock Lake area in order to get as close as possible to the copper-bearing regions, because the mineral had become their chief trade good with the Toltec civilizations of Mexico. Commercial routes traveled by Spiro sailors may even have extended as far as South America. The Andean civilizations of the Chimu and other pre-Inca peoples used copper on a grand scale, although proportionate supplies did not occur in Peru.

Referring to the implements first encountered by Columbus during his fourth voyage to the New World, Drier writes, "That the copper from which these tools, scattered over such a vast area of country, were manufactured, came from the ancient mines of Lake Superior, does not admit of doubt. Although large and numerous deposits of copper ore are scattered through Arizona, New Mexico, Mexico and Central and South America, there is no evidence that the aborigines had sufficient metallurgical knowledge or skill to reduce the ores to refined copper. The shores of Lake Superior have the only known workable deposits of native copper in the world. The term virgin copper is well used to denote its purity. In this latter day, it out-ranks all others in the markets of the world."[36]

Archaeological excavations in the 1930s at Aztalan unearthed the remains of a large, rectangular building containing an abundance of unworked copper, establishing the site's identity as a mining town. A long, broad roll of matting for storage had been thoroughly stained

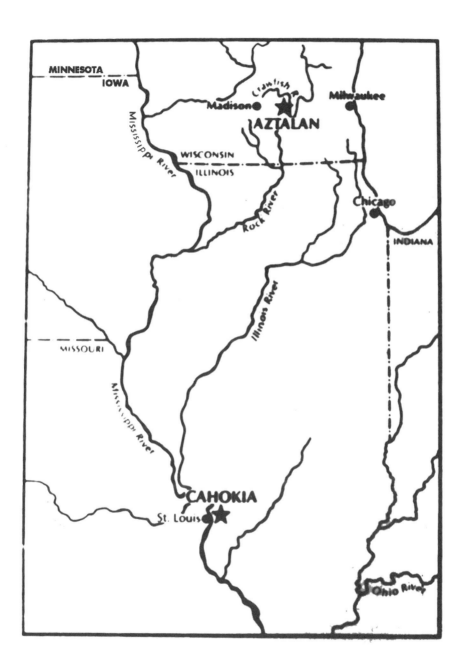

Map showing geographical relationship between Aztalan and Cahokia

with green impregnations from the minerals as they oxidized over time. The building's eight-inch-thick walls were curved slightly and ran between two large furnaces or firepits, all suggesting that the copper was cast into ingots before shipment.[37] As long ago as 1936, so-called "Indian shafts" were observed on the floor of Rock Lake. Again in the early 1990s, divers found several unusually large depressions at the bottom, usually if not always near a stone monument. Although they resemble pits dug by the ancient miners of Isle Royale, their depths are indeterminable, because they are largely filled in with mud and shifting silt. No one has so far been able to define what natural process might be responsible for these strange depressions, which have all the earmarks of manmade features and compare almost exactly in circumference to the Aztalan furnaces or firepits.

A Capital of Empire
The ancient mines explain why a civilization at Rock Lake came about. Tyranena was at the pivot point and crossroads of the prehistoric copper trade. The raw minerals were extracted from the Michigan pits during the short summer season and transported to Rock Lake via the direct river routes that connected the two sites for collection and casting in preparation for shipment.

That the ancient inhabitants of Rock Lake were in fact the same people who mined copper in the Upper Peninsula, there can be little doubt. While no burials exist throughout their vast mining district, around the shores of Rock Lake were more than seventy grave mounds containing the remains of unknown thousands of ancient dead, some interred, many more cremated, and identifiably associated with the prehistoric miners.

Among the best preserved examples were the bones of a man accompanied by a pebble-hammer of the exact kind found throughout Isle Royale. Such tools were used to finish the extracted copper, flattening spurs and trimming off sharp edges. The miner had been buried in a conical earth mound on the south shore of Rock Lake, doubtless like his fellow workers still lying under its waters beneath identical structures of stone.[38] Workers who died on the job in the Michigan copper mines were brought back to be buried in Tyranena's necropolis. Investigators have sought Isle Royale's ancient cemetery for more than a hundred years. They need only look as far as Rock Lake.

If the dates for America's prehistoric mining coincide with the submerged stone structures, the period when operations resumed even more closely fits the life of Aztalan, whose demise took place at the same moment the mines ceased functioning for the last time. But if the Toltecs of Middle America and possibly the Andean civilizers of South America were the Aztalaners' customers in the tenth through fourteenth centuries, who wanted Michigan's copper in far greater quantities more than two thousand years before? The paleo-Indians who sparsely populated the Great Lakes region could have made no demand for the mineral beyond occasional fragments of float copper picked up off the ground, not laboriously mined in six-thousand-pound boulders.

A Superior Technology
Certainly, the most astounding aspects of the Upper Peninsula operations were their vast scope, the prodigious quantities extracted, the advanced procedures of labor organization, shipping, and the actual mining itself, all at a period when the great nations of the earth included Pharaonic Egypt, Trojan Anatolia, Mycenaean Greece, Minoan Crete, and the Hittite Empire of Asia Minor. The American miners were using crib lifts to hoist more than three tons of rock at a time and highly efficient prospecting methods superior to late-eighteenth-century British technology. They were able to cut straight down into sixty feet of solid rock and organized a hierarchy of tasks for thousands of workers. Add to these civilized skills practical astronomy, shipbuilding, and navigation, and we begin to appreciate the greatness of this unknown people. There is, moreover, no indication of a gradual, progressive evolution of all these disciplines and accomplishments in ancient Michigan. They suddenly appeared already fully developed and operational in 3000 B.C., an epoch considered the very dawn of civilization, when only three nations existed on the planet, in the Nile valley, at Mesopotamia's Fertile Crescent, and in the valley of the Indus River. In other words, a society at least on a par with these earliest cultures was already functioning at a feverish pace in the Great Lakes region centuries before the Trojan War.

It is apparent, too, that the miners brought their technology from outside. Development did not take place in the Upper Peninsula. Nothing resembling more than the simplest human societies existed elsewhere in North America at the time. While the ancient miners' identification is the essential question of the Great Copper Mystery, major clues do exist. Their activities in Michigan parallel exactly the European Bronze Age. The American mines shut down the moment that epoch came to a close. One and a half billion pounds of copper extracted from the Upper Peninsula simply disappeared. As DuTemple writes, "Where this copper went is still a mystery."[39] Perhaps it went across the sea to the metal-smiths of pre-Classical Europe, where it was shipped, and the imported Michigan copper was combined with tin and zinc to make bronze.

As Dr. James Scherz, professor of civil engineering at the University of Wisconsin (Madison), asks, "One of the basic questions that hasn't been basically answered yet is, where did all the copper from Lake Superior go? All of the copper found in the mounds, although of a large amount, is but a small percentage of that mined. The Europeans have a complimentary problem. Where did all their copper come from? The Europeans were in a copper trading frenzy from 2000 to 1000 B.C., like we are about oil now, because copper drove their economy."[40]

To be sure, bronze was the most valuable, sought after material, because it was the basis of all weapons production from swords, spear points, and shields to armor, helmets and battering rams. As such, it was really more important and certainly more useful than gold. "The magnitude of the operation (in the Michigan mines) would indicate a strong metallurgically oriented culture," DuTemple concludes. "There was undoubtedly a great economic demand to support this operation with men, materiel, food and transportation. Such effort was probably not put forth to secure copper for trinkets and ornaments, but rather for working tools, probably for armaments and to exchange in trade."[41]

Bronze Age America

To a people for whom bronze was the very basis of their physical culture, sailing regularly to the world's richest copper mines in the Upper Great Lakes was worth the long, dangerous voyage. Indeed, the large-scale transportation of tons of raw copper and additional tons of stone tools to and from Isle Royale across fifty miles of hazardous open water to the nearest shore absolutely necessitates seafarers navigating deep-hull vessels used to rough passage, such as an Atlantic crossing. European sources for tin were Spain and Britain, early referred to as the Cassiterides, or Tin Isles. But their own supplies of copper were too meager to keep the Ancient World in bronze for so many centuries.

Actually, comparison with ancient European mining techniques was noticed as long ago as 1852. The *Annals of Science* reported, "There are also, in the county of Munster, in Ireland, on the Lakes of Kilarny, mines of copper supposed to have been wrought by the

Recreation of Aztalan (north end) as it appeared around 1200 A.D.
from a mural at the Aztalan Historical Museum

Danes, which have shafts three hundred feet deep and which were wrought by the agency of fire. In the same mounds are found hammers or mauls of stone the same as those of Lake Superior, with grooves around the middle."[42]

A more recent piece (1975) in *Compressed Air Magazine* likewise compared Michigan's prehistoric copper miners to those of the British Isles: "They penetrated the earth but a short distance, their deepest workings being equal to those of the old tin mines of Cornwall wrought before the conquest of Britain by the Romans."[43] As mentioned above, it was from Britain, although not exclusively, that Bronze Age metal-smiths obtained tin to combine with copper, so a British resemblance to the Lake Superior mines seems appropriate. In other words, the same prehistoric Europeans were at work in both places, separation by the Atlantic Ocean notwithstanding.

There are also little similitudes of confirming details, such as the vinegar used by the Lake Superior miners to aid spalling, a technique also employed by the miners of ancient Crete.[44] These comparisons are underscored by Indian traditions describing the prehistoric miners as "white men" and "foreigners." And certainly one of the most potent facts supporting Michigan as the prime source for Europe's Bronze Age was the discovery of tin mines among the ancient diggings at Isle Royale. Never used or even recognized by the Plains Indians, tin was combined with copper all over pre-Classical Europe to manufacture bronze.

Rock Lake was the hinge pin of a massive copper mining enterprise and trade network to Europe and the Americas. Without that Wisconsin administrative center, the Bronze Age might not have taken place, at any rate not in the manner it did. Yet, all that remains of these far-flung endeavors to elevate mankind from the Stone Age are still reposing in the twilight depths of Rock Lake.

•3•

Atlantis and the
Copper Question

*For fifty-two years the waters lasted. Thus, they [an ancestral
people] perished. They were swallowed by the waters and their
souls became fish. The heavens collapsed upon them and in a
single day they perished. All the mountains perished (under
the sea).*

—*The Aztec Annals of Cuauhtitlan*

In our search for the lost pyramids of Rock Lake, we have from time
to time inadvertently but inescapably crossed paths with that
greater enigma, the sunken civilization of Atlantis. It is included
here only to throw a bit more light on the Wisconsin mystery, not to
draw any unnecessary parallels that overtax our sense of credibility.
Hence, the point of examining the drowned island-empire will be to
make some sense out of Rock Lake's prehistory.

The earliest known account of Atlantis has been preserved in two
dialogues, the *Timaeus* and the *Critias,* by the Greek philosopher Plato in
the mid-fourth century B.C. He described an Atlantic island beyond the
Straits of Gibraltar, where an imperialist civilization of great affluence
and military might arose to threaten the Mediterranean World. The
Atlanteans marched across North Africa and into Italy against Greece
and Egypt, but were ultimately defeated by Athenian defenders of the
Aegean. At the climax of the war, the island of Atlantis was consumed
by geologic violence and sank into the sea with most of its inhabitants.

Plato's story was expanded by the nineteenth century American "Sage of Ninninger" (Minnesota), Ignatius Donnelly, who concluded that Atlantis was the fountainhead of civilization, whose survivors traveled throughout the world establishing new kingdoms from the Americas to Bronze Age Europe. Donnelly's ideas, once widely accepted, were repudiated by a majority of academics (mostly American) throughout much of the twentieth century, although many first-rank professionals (Thor Heyerdahl, Maria Settegast, Otto Muck, etc.) are beginning to take him seriously again.

Prejudice against Atlantis runs long and deep in the academic community, and not without cause. While Donnelly's innovative tome represented state-of-the-art research in the late nineteenth century, some of its geology, parallel linguistics and relative dating have been savaged in the light of subsequent discoveries made since its 1882 release. Indeed, no scientific opinion may be expected to go unscathed for a hundred years. However, the chief premise of the "Antediluvian World" has been bolstered by the advent of plate tectonics and seafloor spreading. Also, most of its comparative mythologies are no less valid today than the first time Donnelly developed them.

Unfortunately, many of the more than five thousand books and feature articles it spawned tended to discredit all similar research in the eyes of serious investigators, a misfortune that at once condemned responsible Atlantologists to the lunatic fringe of science and prevented interested students from even considering some really vital information about our civilized origins. Having thus thrown the baby out with the bath water, anti-Atlantis scholars have done themselves and their followers a disservice by avoiding the subject as the devil does holy water.

The Atlantis Connection

At any rate, perhaps the most provocative parallel between Rock Lake and Atlantis is the copper trade. As mentioned in the previous chapter, the ancient miners extracted literally millions of pounds of the mineral from the Upper Great Lakes region, beginning around 3000 B.C., concluding their tremendous efforts in the early twelfth century B.C. What became of it all is one of the great mysteries of human prehistory. Coincidentally (?), the North American copper mines flourished at the same time the European Bronze Age was under way. Both stopped together about 1200 B.C. During this 1,800-year epoch, the peoples of Minoan Crete, Mycenaean Greece, the Cycladic Islands, Trojan and Hittite Asia Minor, Villanovan Italy, pre-Celtic Iberia,

*The ancestors of the Aztecs arrive at Vera Cruz
from their island home, Aztlan (i.e., Atlantis)*

from the Codex Mendoza, Archaeological Museum, Mexico City

Britain, and Ireland all manufactured bronze implements, arms and artwork on a stupendous scale—so much so, historians have been hard pressed to locate the sources of copper rich enough to support such a widespread demand. Copper, in fact, was considered so special by the Bronze Age Europeans that the very name "Cyprus" derives from *kipar*, the Assyrian word for copper, because the island was one of the few Mediterranean sources for the mineral. Deposits at Huelva (Spain) and a few other mines scattered throughout Europe were wholly unable to supply the numerous kingdoms which depended upon copper for their survival.

Modern researchers, like Bernard Zangerer, are still puzzled by the Great Copper Mystery: "A new archaeological era began around 3000 B.C. with the first use of bronze in the Aegean. Copper alloys incorporating arsenic had been produced for several centuries in Central Asia, but tin bronze, an alloy of copper and up to 10% tin, was apparently invented away from these early metallurgical centers."[1] The source of that copper invention does not occur in the European World, but the most likely candidate is the Upper Great Lakes region, where copper mining began at the same moment the "new archaeological era" Zangerer mentions got under way.

Atlantis begins to enter the picture when we learn that its existence likewise coincided with the European Bronze Age and the operational life of the Upper Peninsula's ancient copper mines. According to the lunar date given in Plato's dialogues and corroborative Egyptian records, Atlantis was destroyed in the month of the goddess Hathor, or Aethyr (roughly corresponding to our November), 1198 B.C., the same time Michigan's copper mines were abandoned. (The 14,000 B.C. date stated by Plato as the year in which Atlantis sank was an interpreter's error brought about by failing to properly transcompute the Egyptian *lunar* time scale into the Greek *solar* calendar, an oversight left uncorrected since the account was introduced from Egypt to Greece, after 500 B.C.)[2]

As the mercantile middle-men, whose wealth was generated by the copper they mined from the Upper Great Lakes and shipped to European buyers from Ireland to Anatolia, they prized their trade routes to North America as national secrets. After their island capital was obliterated, those secrets were lost and the minerological clearinghouse between the two continents was gone forever. Consequently, the Bronze Age was forced to close, since none of the other, copper-dependent kingdoms knew the location of the Atlanteans' mines, which had been considered a state secret.

We need only compare our society's concern for industrial espionage to understand how the Atlanteans felt about their supplies of copper. Plato additionally described the destruction of Atlantis as having been so cataclysmic, the waters outside the Straits of Gibraltar were impassable because of the thick carpet of volcanic debris that congested the nearby ocean, effectively preventing passage beyond the Mediterranean.[3] Even if the Atlanteans' customers knew about the American copper source, they would not have been able to navigate through miles of geologic residue. Under such impassable conditions, American copper mining was terminated and, with it, the European Bronze Age.

More Valuable Than Gold
Some investigators believe the Bronze Age was naturally superseded by the Iron Age. With the discovery of iron, bronze was supposedly made obsolete. But this viewpoint is patently incorrect, because iron

was widely known and used throughout the civilized world from the Hittite Empire to Old Kingdom Egypt, beyond to Iberia, from the beginning and during the height of their Bronze Age. Moreover, the Bronze Age was not followed by metallurgical advances nor progress of any kind. Quite the contrary, it collapsed into a Dark Age of social chaos and decline that endured for five centuries and blotted out most of the achievements of former times. In many respects, Greeks in the early classical world had to start civilization over again from scratch. Thucydides, the Athenian historian of the fifth century B.C., confidently stated that writing was unknown in Greece before 700 B.C., so complete was the loss of Minoan-Mycenaean literature (Linear-B script) when the Bronze Age ended.[4] It is clear, then, that what rang down the curtain on Bronze Age Europe was not the discovery of iron, but the sudden cutoff of copper supplies.

Plato mentioned that one of the Atlanteans' chief luxury goods was something called "orichalcum." He describes it as among their most important trade items and valued very highly. They even manufactured it in long sheets, with which they decorated their walls and public buildings. Now, orichalcum is nothing less than a particularly high-grade copper ("yellow-copper ore," "brass made from it").[5] And Upper Michigan, as we learned, is the world's greatest source for the metal. Combined with the Atlanteans' reputation as ocean-going sailors, the identity of the white-skinned "Marine Men," as the Menomonie remember them, seems less doubtful.

Plato, in fact, portrayed the Atlanteans as busy, skilled miners. Moreover, Michigan's prehistoric copper operations—with their miles of deep pits and ore extracted in hundreds of thousands of tons—are on the same colossal scale he said belonged to the people of Atlantis, where their feats of irrigation and canal construction were equally gargantuan. As Donnelly asked more than a hundred years ago, "Who carried vast quantities of copper, tin and bronze to Denmark, Norway, Sweden, Ireland, England, France, Spain, Switzerland and Italy? Where can we find them, save in that people of Atlantis, whose ships, docks, canals and commerce provoked the astonishment of the ancient Egyptians, as recorded by Plato?"[6]

Not a Myth!

That the mysterious miners of the Upper Great Lakes Region were Atlanteans responsible for the European Bronze Age is by no means a novel concept. Even before Donnelly published his magnum opus about the antediluvian world, scholars, perhaps less intimidated by academic dogma, recognized some inescapable parallels between America's prehistoric copper mining enterprise and the story of Atlantis. Among the most prominent of those investigators was Edward Herbert Thompson, the doyen of Mesoamerican studies in the early decades of the twentieth century and the first modern excavator of Chichen Itza, the Mayas' great ceremonial center in Yucatan. While at the Worcester Polytechnic Institute in Massachusetts in 1879, he published "Atlantis not a Myth," in *Popular Science Monthly*.[7] The article caused a sensation in the professional community and, in his words, won him "the attention of several influential men who were interested in archaeological research."

Thompson wrote of the destruction of Atlantis: "It is not to be supposed that all perished in that calamity. Long before this, they had spread over the portion of the Americas contiguous to the peninsula, building cities, palaces, roads and aqueducts like those of their native home; and adventurous pioneers were continually spreading north, east and westward, their constant increase of numbers from their former homes enabling them to overcome the resistance offered to their progress by both natives and nature, until they at last reached and discovered the copper country of Lake Superior. That they appreciated this discovery is evinced by the innumerable evidences of their works and of their skill in discovering the richest and most promising veins. Wherever our miners of the present day go, they find their ancient fellow workmen have been there before them, worked the richest veins and gathered the best copper; and it is supposed that they continued thus till the terrible blotting-out of their native country cut short all this, and left this advancing civilization to wither and die like a vine severed from the parent stem.

"Having no further accession to their numbers and being continually decimated by savages and disease, they slowly retreated before the ever-advancing hordes. Gradually, and contesting every step, as is shown by their numerous defensive works along their path, they were forced back to their cities on this continent, that had been spared them from the universal destruction of their country, where the dense and almost impassable forests afforded them their last refuge from their enemies and where, reduced by war, pestilence and other causes to a feeble band, their total extinction was only a matter of time. Such is probably the history of this lost civilization and such would have been the history of our own civilization had we in our infant growth been cut off from receiving the nourishment of the mother countries."

Thompson's conclusions were not pure speculation but based partly on native American tradition, which recounted that the ancient copper miners were the Marine Men, or men of the ocean, a sea people, mostly wiped out by the ancestors of the Attwandeton and Chippewa, whose souls sank back into the sea.[8] The Indian tribal accounts do indeed seem to echo an Atlantean presence in America, even to the collapse of Atlantis and its people into an oceanic catastrophe. Algonkian tribes in the Great Lakes Region recalled that their cult-hero, Nanabozho, supervised the recreation of the world after the Flood, which he survived by riding on a big "wooden raft," along with animals he took on board, just like Noah, although the Algonkian tradition predates the Biblical version's introduction to America by unguessed generations.[9]

Native Americans Recall Atlantis
Even more overtly Atlantean were the oral accounts of the resident Winnebagoes, whose Siouan ancestors traded animal hides and meat with the twelfth century lords of Aztalan. In their Worak, or tribal histories, they tell of ancient origins in the Wolf Clan, whose leader dwelt in "a great lodge" on an island in the ocean where the sun rises. This progenitor had ten sons, one of whom came to Turtle Island (North America) with his clansmen and women. In time, they intermarried with the natives and established four new clans: the White Wolf, Green Hair, Gray Wolf, and Black Wolf. The quartet was so named to commemorate the Four Cardinal Directions which streamed out from their oceanic homeland at the center of the world. The first child born in this new land was called "Wave," after the bow-wave of the boat that brought them from the great lodge.

In an alternate version, "the original Wolf brothers appeared from the bottom of the ocean," where their ancestral island had been swallowed up by a terrible deluge. As the disturbed seas began to calm down, the Wakt'cexi, a water-spirit, arose from the waves wearing a horned helmet and led the survivors across the ocean on improvised rafts to the new land. Thereafter, all the Wolf clans were known as Water clans.

Paul Radin writes (1923), "There may be some significance in the origin legends of some of the clans which claim that they came from over the sea, but it is utterly impossible to determine whether we are here dealing with a myth pure and simple or with a vague memory of some historical happening."[10] Curiously, many academic scholars normally discount a people's own tradition of the past as "a myth pure and simple." Yet who should know better what took place than they?

The Horned Giant

As though to confirm the Winnebago story of the horned Wakt'cexi, two effigy mounds of gigantic proportions may be found in Wisconsin. They represent the water spirit that led the Wolf Clan ancestors of the Winnebago from the Great Flood. One of the geoglyphs still exists, although in mutilated form, on the slope of a hill in Greenfield Township, outside Baraboo, only forty-five miles from Rock Lake. Road construction cut off the legs below his knees earlier this century, but the figure is otherwise intact. The giant is 214 feet long and thirty feet across at the shoulders. His anthropomorphic image is oriented westward, as though walking from the east and the Flood that drowned "the great lodge." His horned helmet identifies him as the Wakt'cexi deluge-hero. The terraglyph is no primitive work, but beautifully proportioned and formed. Increase Lapham, the renowned surveyor who measured the man-mound in the early nineteenth century, was impressed: "All the lines of this most singular effigy are curved gracefully and much care has been bestowed upon its construction."[11]

A companion of the Greenfield Township hill-figure, also in Sauk County, about thirty miles northwest, was drowned under several fathoms of river by a dam project in the early twentieth century. Ironically, the water spirit which led the Winnebagoes' ancestors from a catastrophic flood has itself become the victim of another deluge.

The Atlantean identity of the Wakt'cexi and his Wisconsin effigy mounds is repeated in his overseas' counterpart, the Long Man of Wilmington. It, too, is the representation of a man (at 300 feet, the largest in Europe) cut into the chalk face of a hill in the south of England. It is dated to the last centuries of Atlantis (from 2000 to 1200 B.C.) and is positioned very similarly to the Wisconsin man-mound, even to its westward orientation. The resemblance grows closer, however, when we learn that the British hill-figure was originally portrayed wearing a horned helmet that was obliterated in the early nineteenth century. Since the Long Man of Wilmington and the Wisconsin man-mounds are the only examples of their kind in the world, it does not beggar our credibility to regard the New and Old World effigies as products of a single people, probably representing a com-

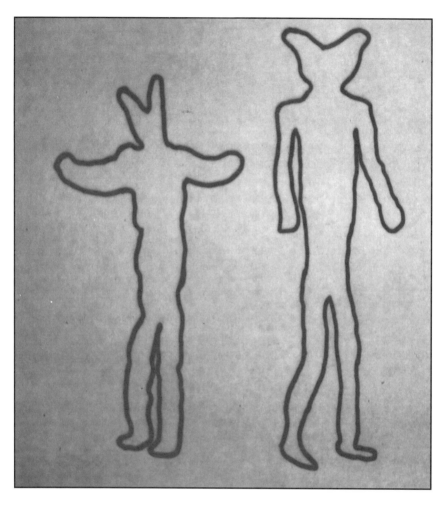

Surveyor's drawing of the two Wisconsin effigy mounds portraying the "Water Spirit" who came to America after the Great Flood. At left, the Baraboo Man-Mound, Right, the La Valle figure that was destroyed by the waters of a dam.

mon theme; namely, the migration of survivors from the Atlantis cataclysm led by men whose mark of authority was the horned helmet.

While the North American man-mounds occur only in Wisconsin, the horned figure they depict was known to historic tribes as far away as the West Coast. A child initiation ceremony employed by the Navaho involved a masked figure wearing a red wig and a horned helmet accompanied by a woman, her face painted white, portraying

his wife. They were supposed to represent the couple which survived
the Great Flood as a reminder of the child's ancestral origins.[12] The
horned helmet is obvious enough, and the couple's depicted racial
identity re-emphasizes their Atlantean derivation. Interestingly,
numerous mythic traditions around the world, from Africa to Polyne-
sia, remember the Atlanteans as red-headed.[13]

Apaches of Atlantis

This theme of a horned figure in connection with ancestral beginnings
following a terrible deluge in the Eastern Sea was known in fascinating
variations across North America and is celebrated among a few tribes
even today. In the Apache Crown Dance, performers join in a circle
around a "speaker" wearing a horned headgear, at the center of which
is the stylized representation of an erupting volcano. As though this
ancient accouterment were not too apparent, he wields a trident, the
emblem of Poseidon, the mythic founder of Atlantis. The speaker
thrusts it into the ground, then begins, "I remember the Old Red Land,"
a narration describing Apache origins after some oceanic catastrophe.[14]

Like the Navaho tradition, the color red figures in noticeably, perhaps because the island of Atlantis itself was largely red due to its
great quantities of tufa. In fact, Plato wrote that the predominant natural colors of Atlantis were red, white, and black—identifying the
minerals typical of a volcanic island: tufa, pumice, and lava, respectively. These colors also make up the ceremonial costume of the
Crown Dancer. Appropriately, the Apaches belong to the Wolf Clan,
the same totem described above in Siouan traditions as the water
spirit who led flood survivors to America from the east.15

The impact of Atlantis reverberated as far as California, where
the remarkable Chumash made their home in what is now the Santa
Barbara area. There they created the most colorful and vibrant cave
paintings, in which the horned water spirit figured prominently.
Referred to as Dancing Frog, the red-white-black image called upon
the ancestral powers of ancient forebears, who brought their magic
with them from the Great Lodge before it sank into the Eastern Sea.

The Chumash alone preferred to work in the identifiably Atlantean
tricolor, and, although they were inadvertently exterminated by the
white man's diseases against which they had no immunity, they left
behind numerous images in their cave art which suggest old ties to
Atlantis. These include concentric circles (recalling the alternating
rings of land and water Plato said comprised the layout of the

Atlantean capital); redundant variations of the cross, often within a circle (signifying Atlantis as the cultural Navel of the World); and the swastika, the emblem of the sun in Atlantean religion.

Symbols specifically connecting the Chumash with Atlantis through the Canary Islands, from which the first civilizers of Rock Lake came around 3000 B.C., were found in cave paintings depicting a pair of circles linked by a vertical line. In Tenerife, largest of the Canary Islands, where this sign was identically etched into caves by the Guanches, the ancient inhabitants of the island, it signified a solar position, the same meaning it probably had for the native American artists, because it appears surrounded by other astronomical glyphs.[16]

The Chumash were themselves unique among the other indigenous tribes. The Spaniards referred to them as "superior Indians" for their relatively refined culture, beautiful women, and courteous behavior, all of which was in sharp contrast to the mountain tribes of the interior, who gave the conquistadors a rough welcome. More remarkably, the Chumash were physically different from the rest of the continent's aboriginal inhabitants. Among a beardless population, they alone grew substantial facial hair. Santa Cruz, a major Chumash settlement, was called the "Island of the Bearded Indians" by the early Spanish missionaries. Photographs of one of the last pure-blood Chumash, taken in 1878, show a man in his mid-30s sporting a thick mustache and bushy sideburns. His profile appears singularly non-Amerindian, while a full frontal view of the face suggests someone of mixed ancestry.[17] Were the Chumash descendants of unions between a native people and voyagers from Atlantis?

Radiocarbon tests of their rock art have dated occupation of the area to 950 B.C., plus or minus a hundred years, which puts the Chumash artists in the same time frame for the years immediately following the destruction of Atlantis.[18] Their possible Atlantean origins were underscored by the Chumash material culture, which was absolutely unique in native America for its maritime richness. The Bearded Indians built and sailed *tomols,* wooden ships in excess of twenty-four feet long, with four-foot-plus beams, which regularly navigated sixty-five-mile runs to San Nicolas Island from the mainland. Described by the leading researcher of the Chumash as their "finest technological achievement," "unique in the New World," the tomols were constructed of wood planks waterproofed with asphalt and therefore similar to the ships manned by the horn-helmeted Sea Peo-

Medinet Habu as it appeared during its final
phase of construction, about 1180 B.C.
diorama reconstruction at Milwaukee Public Museum

ples portrayed on the walls of the Victory Temple of Rameses III, in
Upper Egypt, discussed below.[19] The Spaniards, who were the foremost seamen of the world in the sixteenth century, had only high
praise for the tomols' speed and seaworthiness.

Atlanteans in California

The Chumash were themselves a kind of sea people, in that their well-
built houses were made to resemble ships, while canoes were used for
burials. Even their leaders were not referred to as "chiefs," but as
"captains."[20] Their term for "ship"—tomol—is the same word for
"pine," from which the vessels were made.[21] Their villages were near
the sea, while all the pictographic caves are in close proximity to water.
And some intriguing connections may be followed from the Chumash
through Atlantis to ancient Egypt. At least a dozen of the pictographs
among the Chumash rock paintings resemble and, in many cases,
duplicate Egyptian hieroglyphs. These include symbols for water,
stars, mountains, rudders, heaven, eternity, town, day, alive, etc.

Shield-bearing Atlanteans with horned helmets, as portrayed 3,200 years ago on the walls of the Victory Temple of Rameses III (Medinet Habu)

The list is long enough and comparison of the petroglyphs and hieroglyphs close enough to argue for contact between these two vastly separated peoples. After all, the Chumash were painting these symbols on the walls of California's caves at the same time Egyptians were decorating the tombs and temples of the Nile Valley with, in some instances, identical hieroglyphic signs. Nor does the comparison end here.

The Chumash envisioned the destructive power of the sun as a ferocious lioness, the same imagery used by the Egyptians to portray the sun's negative aspects. Not only were these solar interpretations identical, the names for both were similar enough to make investigators suspect a common root-word. The Chumash deity was called Sok-so-uh; Sekh-au-tet was the Egyptian goddess.[22] Even closer to the point of our comparison, the very name "Chumash" may be the missing link to Atlantis through Egypt. It derives from Tchumac, or "People of the Island," and echoes Shu, the Egyptian version of Atlas himself, the eponymous king of the island of Atlantis.[23]

This is not to argue that the Chumash were Egyptians, or that ancient sailors from the Nile Valley somehow reached the west coast of America. If nothing else, the plank construction of the redoubtable tomols owes more to the thirteenth-century-B.C. Sea Peoples than to Egyptian design. Rather, the Chumash and the Egyptians, forever separated by half a world, were both impacted by Atlantean culture-bearers, who shared with both peoples elements of writing, maritime technology, and even their genes. The hieroglyphs and solar lion-goddess concept developed in the Old Red Land were brought by survivors of its oceanic disaster into the Nile Valley and, eventually, to the shores of what is now southern California.

While these "Egyptian" parallels are provocative in themselves, they become even more impressive when we consider certain cultural elements of the Chumash which point to overseas, and particularly Atlantean, connections, such as their seafaring proficiency, beards among an otherwise beardless population, the choice of Atlantean colors for their most sacred artworks, the horned Dancing Frog from the Great Flood, etc. It was their common gifts from Atlantis that account for so many remarkable correspondences between the Chumash and the Ancient Egyptians.

Numerous Atlantean themes likewise permeate the tribal account of the Winnebago Wolf Clan. The "great lodge" on an island in the Atlantic Ocean is obvious enough. According to Plato, Atlantis was the center of the world, a location affirmed by the four colors of the clans corresponding to the cardinal directions, which spread from the island. In the *Critias,* we read that Poseidon, the sea god who created Atlantis, sired ten sons to rule as monarchs over the various territories of his empire, just as the Winnebago account mentions ten sons fathered on the island by their great ancestor.[24]

The sinking of this ancestral island is obvious, too, but the identity of the horned water spirit, celebrated from Wisconsin's man-mound to the Chumash rock art of California, is no less amazing. The Egyptians of the Twenty-first Dynasty portrayed the Sea Peoples, with whom they fought several major engagements in the early twelfth century B.C., as warriors wearing horned helmets. The Victory Temple of Pharaoh Rameses III in the Upper Nile Valley of the Kings is the best preserved of its kind in Egypt, and on its walls the visitor may still see relief sculpture of his armies battling the Sea People's marines, clearly portrayed with horned helmets on their heads.

Defeat of the Sea Peoples

Now, the testimony of these captured invaders from the sea reveals they were the same marauding Atlanteans described by Plato. They told Pharaoh's interrogators that their homeland, known to the Egyptians as "Netero" (a "holy island," similarly characterized by Plato), "beyond the 12th Bow" (in the Distant West), had been overwhelmed by a natural catastrophe and drowned in the ocean.[25] The horned effigies in Wisconsin's Sauk County were fashioned to represent the Wakt'cexi, the same helmeted flood survivors depicted on the walls of the Victory Temple of Rameses dedicated to the defeat of invaders from Atlantis.

That these capable seafarers could have had easy access to the copper mining region of the Upper Great Lakes there is no doubt. Octave DuTemple, cited in the previous chapter, showed that the Upper Peninsula mining regions were easily accessible from the Atlantic coast during the centuries of the European Bronze Age: "Approximately 3,500 years ago, the post-glacial Great Lakes were in the Lake Nipissing Stage. Lakes Superior, Michigan and Huron were all at 605-foot elevations above sea-level. At this time, it was possible to travel east directly to the oceans via North Bay and the Ottawa River, and thence out the St. Lawrence to the sea, or south via Chicago, Des Plaines and the Mississippi River. The route over Niagara Falls was also open."[26]

*Trojan carrying ox-hide copper ingot, as portrayed in
a bronze incense burner found in the sea off Cyprus*

.4.

Atlanteans Take Over America

Where was I? I had to know. I wanted to speak. I wanted to tear off the copper helmet enclosing my head. But Captain Nemo came over and took me by the arm. He then picked up a piece of chalky stone and went over to a rock of black basalt, where he wrote only a single word: Atlantis.

—Jules Verne
20,000 Leagues Under the Sea

A mong the most startling and convincing pieces of physical evidence linking the Americas, and particularly those parts of the continent concerning the Rock Lake phenomenon, with Bronze Age Europe, through Atlantis, are the metal ox hides found on both sides of the Atlantic Ocean.

Pre-Classical metal smiths in the Mediterranean world cast copper ingots into a rectangular form resembling the hide of a skinned ox. The configuration not only allowed for practical storage, particularly in the holds of transport ships, but permitted easy portage over the shoulder, while the four "legs" were handles for pairs of dock stewards, facilitating on-off loading. A Cypriot stand for a bronze incense burner appropriately depicts a man (his turned-up shoes and long robes identify him as a Trojan or certainly an inhabitant of some coastal Anatolian civilization) handling a copper ox hide.[1] Indeed, whole cargoes of identically shaped ingots have been salvaged in modern times, most commonly off the coasts of Turkey and

Crete. The Cape Gelidonya wreck, with its thirty-four ox hide ingots, was undoubtedly a Bronze Age merchantman, but an even older example is on display at Iraklion's Archaeological Museum, where the original copper ox hide shipment from a sunken Minoan vessel is wonderfully preserved after more than thirty-five centuries. The ox hide was used simultaneously by every European people who traded in bronze. It was a standardized, universally recognized design not associated with any nation in particular, although exclusively connected with the transportation and storage of bronze and copper ingots until the twelfth century B.C.

Remarkably, an identically shaped copper ox hide presently at the Museo Arqueologico de la Serena was found tied to the forearm of a human skeleton excavated below the Coquimbo Cemetery, on the north-central coast of Chile.[2] Its discovery there was no accident. Copper mining still goes on near La Serena, its roadstead and docking area. The natural harbor is among the best sheltered in Chile, continuing to serve as a loading point for copper, even as a winter haven for the Chilean navy.

Doubtless these revealing features were no less accommodating in the ancient past, when other navies shipped the same ore from La Serena. The Coquimbo find is by no means unique, however, and belongs to the Canari, the Ecuadoran sea traders in copper described in *The Lost Pyramids of Rock Lake*. The American Canari produced and handled a copper currency known to the Spaniards as *hachuelas*, or "axe-monies," in the shapes of axe heads, mushrooms and ox hides. Examples by the kilogram have been found and many are today preserved in private collections or public museums throughout Peru, Ecuador, and Mexico.

Proof in Copper
Closer to the focus of our investigation, a sixty-pound copper ox hide was discovered near Lake Gogebic, in Michigan's Upper Peninsula.[3] The Michigan State Museum in Lansing displays a much smaller ox-hide-shaped stone anciently used as a medium of exchange similar to the Canari *hachuelas*.[4] Other examples occur at Ohio's Humerechouse Museum in Coshocton, while a petroglyph incised on a natural rock face at Peterborough, Ontario, clearly depicts an ox hide of the kind that was carried by copper miners and shippers 3,500 years ago.[5] Such abundant material evidence from the Mediterranean and the Americas unquestionably establishes a Bronze Age presence here,

particularly among the contemporary copper mines of Michigan's Upper Peninsula.

Old World connections with the Americas in pre-Columbian times are numerous, but those which clearly link Rock Lake and the Aztalaners with the Aztecs, their immediate descendants, to events in Bronze Age Europe through Atlantis make for provocative investigation. Among the most intriguing examples is the sacred bundle, a mystical religious object revered by holy men and their cult followers. In Greek myth, Helenus was a Trojan soothsayer who was able to predict the future and perform other psychic feats by means of a black, oblong stone known as the Ophitis, or Serpent Stone. He wrapped it in a bundle of swaddling clothes, like an infant's garments, and offered it arcane sacrifices and occult incantations until "a living presence warmed the precious substance."[6]

This special object may have been the Palladium, the most sacrosanct, spiritually potent artifact in Ilios, the Trojan capital, and stolen away by Odysseus after the city fell to his wooden horse. Remarkably, the same sacred bundle appeared among the Aztecs as a black stone wrapped in cloth to represent Texcatlipocha, and provided predictions of future events.[7] The identical character of both Trojan and Aztec religious bundles rules out any possible coincidence.

Shamans belonging to the Midewiwin, the Grand Medicine Lodge of the Great Lakes, were entrusted with a sacred bundle containing a seashell resembling the one that appeared to the Ojibwa out of the eastern ocean and led them to the west. Here a connection to Atlantean origins is apparent, a connection made many centuries earlier and far to the south, at Yucatan, among the Mayas, whose demise predated the Aztec state by four centuries. They, too, asserted that their forefathers arrived in Middle America from over the sunrise sea, and that they carried a sacred bundle containing a special stone, the Giron-Gagel.[8] It had been entrusted to their ancestral leader as "a symbol of power and majesty."

The sacred bundle is represented in Mayan hieroglyphs as a knot wrapped in a fishnet, recalling its mythic origins in the sea. Even the mineral of the black stones was common to all the cultures in question. Helenus's Ophitis was actually obsidian, just as "Texcatlipocha" means literally "Mirror of Obsidian," which was, in fact, the stone enclosed in his sacred bundle.[9] So, too, the Trojan Serpent Stone is repeated in the Aztec representation of Texcatlipocha as a manifestation of the Plumed Serpent, Quetzalcoatl.

The Trojan Question

While the physical evidence for a European Bronze Age impact on prehistoric America seems clear, we should not mistake Trojan for Atlantean remains. Archaeologists have uncovered traces in Atlantic Spain supposedly left by Trojan culture-bearers, but the total lack of any other allegedly "Trojan" artifacts between Iberia and Anatolia casts more than a little doubt on the assumed identity of the Spanish finds.[10] They occur, after all, within the Atlantean, not the Trojan sphere of influence.

Troy, although a powerful maritime nation, was not large enough to expand its influence beyond the Bosporus and the Ionian Sea. Rather, the Trojans were themselves an Atlantean people, belonging to one of the cultural outposts of Atlantis, as recalled in their own foundation-myth of Dardanus. He was the son of Electra, herself a daughter of Atlas (literally, an "Atlantis"), who sent him away from her sinking island. The Atlantean character of Troy has been examined in greater depth than this volume allows, but it is important for our present understanding of European Bronze Age influences in pre-Columbian America that we see them as Atlantean rather than Anatolian in origin.[11]

"Trojan" (i.e., Atlantean) themes abound throughout Meso-america, but one of cogent significance to our investigation concerns the late classic coastal city of Tulum, in Yucatan. As we shall discover in a forthcoming chapter, a small contingent of culture-bearers left this ceremonial center to found Aztalan, in the early twelfth century A.D. It was the only Maya settlement to be enclosed by a rectangular wall, a feature that gave the whole complex a strong resemblance to its Wisconsin counterpart and was responsible for its name.

In Quiche, the language spoken by the Lowland Maya, *tu* means "to go around"; hence *Tulum* signifies "that which goes around a place," or simply "the Enclosure." "Tu" was also used by the Mayas to describe some of their astronomical calculations, and it is this astronomical aspect of *tu* that makes for a compelling comparison with the ancient world in the Bronze Age. "Tur" was known to the Trojans as their name for the Pole Star, "around" which the heavens revolved.[12] Thus, *tu* not only has the same meaning in both Quiche and Trojan, but had an astronomical application in both cases.

The Atlantean-Trojan connection with America's Mississippian culture also includes a shocking piece of physical evidence found among the archaeological digs at Angel Mounds during the 1930s.

Scene at Tulum: El Castillo from the northwest watchtower

Retrieved from Aztalan's sister city in southern Indiana was a pair of boar tusks. Like Aztalan, Angel Mounds was a pyramidal ceremonial center enclosed behind a stockaded wall of plastered lime and lorded over by astronomer-priests who left the super-city at Cahokia about A.D. 1100 to resettle with their followers on the banks of the Ohio River, at today's Evansville. Of course, boars were not native to America prior to the Spanish arrival, so the most elementary reason must conclude that the tusks are material proof of a European presence in pre-Columbian Indiana.

But establishment archaeologists, to whom the merest hint of Old World influences in America during prehistoric times is heresy, speculated that a caravan of swine traveling in Hernando DeSoto's sixteenth-century expedition across the prairie dropped their tusks along the trail, where they were picked up by the Indians, who decided to bury them at Angel Mounds![14] This ludicrous scenario cooked up to cover doubts about pre-Columbian transatlantic contacts is certainly harder to swallow than the possibility of a European arrival in the Mississippi Valley long before DeSoto.

Far more importantly, the Angel Mounds boar tusks form another significant piece of the archaeological puzzle defining a Midwest relationship with Bronze Age sailors. Boar tusks were used in the making of ceremonial helmets worn by Trojan warriors of high rank. At least one such helmet and several representations in pre-Classical Aegean art still exist.[14] They validate Homer's description of identical thirteenth century B.C. headgear in the *Iliad*.

Another boar-tusk helmet was on the head of an idol venerated in the Aztalan-like cities throughout the Mississippi Valley. The seated, cross-legged figure's decidedly non-Amerindian facial features contributed to its "foreign" appearance.[15] The existence of this otherwise entirely unique helmet design exclusive to the Bronze Age Aegean World, yet occurring in America's Mississippi Culture, is not as problematical as it may seem.

In the popular film, *Dances with Wolves*, a mid-nineteenth century Sioux elder possessed a conquistador's helmet from Spanish contacts made four hundred years before. Such preservation from generation to generation among native Americans was an accurate portrayal of the perpetual veneration of sacred or otherwise important objects treasured as tribal heirlooms. The Trojan-like helmets were no less preserved and revered, as shown by the idol's Bronze Age headgear and the anomalous boar tusks from Angel Mounds.

Illustration made by an artist with Hernando De Soto in his expedition across the southern United States in the sixteenth century. The drawing depicts an ancestor-idol set up in the temples of various tribes. Note its un-Indian cast of facial features and distinctive headgear.

Mycenaean stone relief of a Greek warrior at the time of the Trojan War (circa 1250 B.C.), depicted with a helmet made of boar tusks

Ivory statuette of a Greek warrior wearing a
boar-tusk helmet at the time of the Trojan War

National Museum, Athens, Greece

Modern replica of Greek armor at the time of the Trojan War.
Note the helmet made of boar tusks.

National Museum, Athens, Greece

Actual ox-hide copper ingots from a Trojan wreck
Bodrum Museum in Turkey

The Bronze Age Arrives in South America

Although a thorough presentation of evidence for Bronze Age contacts in Middle America is outside the purview of our Rock Lake investigation, at least one particularly cogent parallel merits attention. Mention was made of the axe-shaped stone and copper currency that was traded from the Upper Great Lakes to Chile in pre-Columbian times. Several such examples found in Ecuador were double-headed axes. These were especially revealing finds, in that the twin-bladed hatchet is the labrys, the emblem of the "Sacred Duality" mystery cult.

The best-known practice of this mystery was in Minoan Crete from about 2000 to 1500 B.C., but it was likewise known in Troy and throughout the Aegean World. The professional establishment's response after the South American discovery was immediate and typical: "A suggestion of a double axe is out of place in Ecuadoran archaeology."[16]

When such finds are not made by a university-trained expert, they are almost invariably and instantly branded as "fakes." But when one of their own stumbles upon cultural anomalies, they are made to fit into the mold of preconceived opinion. Out of place the artifacts may be, but three of the leading authorities on axe monies (Horido Shimada, Robert Bennett, and Eric Pedersen) described the Ecuadoran currency in question as "double-T" in configuration.[17] These South American examples and the double axes on display at Iraklion's Archaeological Museum in Crete undoubtedly sprang from the same concept.

Heather Lechtman writes (1990), "The axe was an important symbol of power in western Mexico and elsewhere in Mesoamerica, with ritual and ceremonial functions. The ethno-historic evidence she [Hosler] assembled is clear about the symbolic, ritual and political use of the axe in Mexican society."[18] Lechtman's description matches everything that is known about the Cretan double axe. As though additional evidence were necessary, both the Minoan and Ecuadoran specimens are made of copper. The labrys in South America is but another credible and significant proof of a Bronze Age presence during pre-Columbian times.

Mud Lake's rabbit-shaped earthwork, immediately south of Rock Lake, is unmistakably defined as a lunar symbol by its companion crescent-moon mound. Similarly, the Aztecs associated the moon with a hare, the same creature identified as a servant of Artemis, the lunar goddess, in the Old World tale of Cadmus. In *The Lost Pyramids of Rock Lake*, a chapter describes Cadmus' journey to the Isles of the Blest, known today as the Canary Islands, off the coast of North Africa. Here, too, material evidence supports legend.

On the Canary Island of La Palma are the Belmaco Inscriptions, near Maco, Barranco de las Zarzas, and Fuente de la Zarza, where the best preserved sacred spiral petroglyphs may still be seen. The spiral was the leading emblem of the ancient Wisconsinites, in Aztalan, and practically the national symbol of Atlantis, which was itself configured like a huge spiral.[19] Nor was it the only sign common to both the prehistoric Canary Islanders and the Aztalaners. The Guanche or Canari ceramic stamps used to tattoo arms and faces included the circle-within-the-triangle, triangle-within-a-circle, or triangle-within-a-triangle. These singular and otherwise unique designs were also found at Wisconsin's Rice Lake, source for the catlinite imported for ritual use atop Aztalan's Pipestone Hill in Aztalan itself and at her sister city in Indiana, Angel Mounds.

There are also some provocative cognates linking the speech of the ancient Americans with the Canary Islander language, Guanche. The form "Gua" is a nominative prefix occurring in "Guanche," "Guarteme" (the title of a Canary Island ruler), "Guadfra" (the daughter of

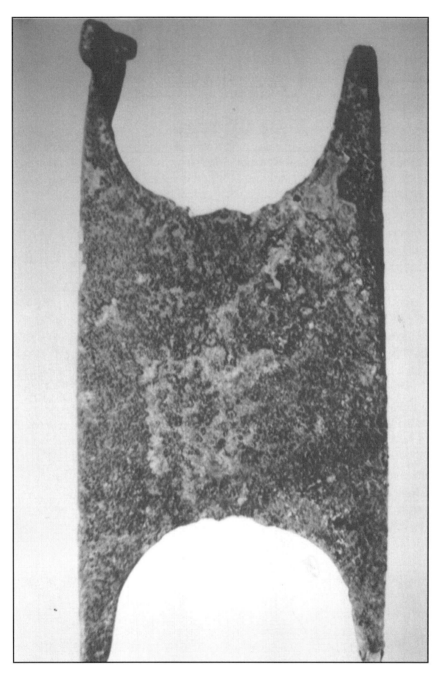

Pre-Inca ox-hide copper ingot
from Chile

Lanzarote's last native king), etc. It recurs, appropriately enough, among Ecuador's Canari, the great seafarers who shipped goods for the Aztec Empire and whose name is identical to the Atlantic Islanders under discussion. Among these Mesoamericans appear "Guayaqui" (one of their major ceremonial cities), "Guapan" (site of a Canari tomb that yielded 736 kilograms of copper axe monies) and "Guacri-caur" (the second king to rule the upper coastal plains of South America). With Guacri-caur, our trail of evidence leads inevitably back to origins in Atlantis. His father was a culture-hero known throughout the pre-Inca world, Taycanamo, who arrived at American shores "on a balsa raft" with a commission from "a great lord across the sea" to govern the natives.[20]

Evidence for an Atlantean presence in the Canary Islands is profuse and could easily comprise a book or two of its own. Here, it must suffice only to touch on the highlights of that neglected material. Foremost are the oral traditions of the original Guanche inhabitants, who recalled the story of Atlantis for Roman visitors in the first century B.C.[21] The Guanches' leading deity was Atua, envisioned as a giant holding up the sky, just as the eponymous monarch of Atlantis, Atlas, was represented as a titan bearing the vault of heaven on his shoulders.[22] Both the names and functions of these two figures identify them as the same god.

Among the Guanches' petroglyphs still found throughout Gran Canaria are several depictions of Atua-Atlas. In fact, John Harms writes (1965) that Mt. Teide, the 12,200-foot volcano of Tenerife, was "also known as Atlas to the Ancients." Teide itself may have been created by the same natural catastrophe that destroyed Atlantis: "Geophysicists see evidence of the crater's origin in the sinking of a big mountain and perhaps rise at the same time as the result of some primeval cataclysm."[23]

In Greek myth, Atlas dwelt on an island, at the center of which was the Garden of the Hesperides, who were four daughters he had by Hespera, goddess of the evening star. They tended the Tree of Life, which was inhabited by Ladon, a guardian dragon. In Roman records and even in modern references, the Canary Islands are known as "the Hesperides." And they do indeed feature a Dragon Tree—several, in fact—and its healing properties, like the not-entirely-mythical Tree of Life, have been valued for centuries.

The modern *draena draco*, among the oldest living trees in the world, clearly derives from the old story of Ladon, its guardian dragon. Today's medicinal *draena draco* is his Tree of Life in the Canary Islands' Garden of the Hesperides, where dwelt the king of Atlantis, Atlas.

The Canary Islands were certainly part of the Atlantean Empire and they may have belonged to the blood-related kingdom of Diaprepes, the twin brother of Atlas, mentioned by Plato in the *Critias*. His name, the Shining One, is a reference to lunar worship, which was manifest in the Canaries.[24] There, the priest-kings bore the title, Guanarteme, from Artemis, the Greek goddess of the moon, whose name in the Canari title demonstrates a surprising connection between the Aegean World and the Atlantic. We are reminded, too, of Rock Lake's Temple of the Moon, Aztalan's Pyramid of the Moon, and the lunar symbols discovered in the area.

The Disaster
When the mining officials at ancient Rock Lake learned of the catastrophe that had obliterated their distant island home, they must have realized their work could not continue and that their lives in this far country were over. They abandoned the settlement and buried their sacred monuments under ten fathoms of water channeled from a tributary of the Rock River. Was that deed a premeditated deluge, a deliberate reenactment of the natural disaster that had just dragged their great capital to the bottom of the ocean? Perhaps it was an act of sympathetic magic, wherein the souls of their honored dead entombed on the shores of Rock Lake were sent to join in like manner their drowned kinsmen in Atlantis.

There is yet another compelling comparison with the end of Atlantis. In my long search for viable contacts with the native Americans' title for Rock Lake, Tyranena, I found a name it resembled both phonetically and symbolically. It belongs to the Old Irish language, with origins predating the Celts by centuries. Is it an Atlantean carryover? In any case, it is part of the prehistoric flood-tradition in Ireland, the story of Tir-nan 'og, "the Land beneath the Sea."

An especially interesting link between America's Mississippi Culture and Ireland through Atlantis appears in the figure of Lugh, the pre-Celtic fire god, who left his name to several towns and cities across Britain and the European continent, including Lyon, Leyden, and the Roman Lughballium (today's Carlisle). After the Christian takeover of Ireland, Lugh and his followers were banished to the heathen Underworld, where they survive in folklore as the leprechaun (from Lugh Chromain, or "Little Stooping Lugh"). He was the grandson of Balor, king of the Underwater People, the Formorach, who invaded Ireland from their island-empire fortress in the middle of the Atlantic Ocean.

Lugh became the leader of another Atlantean Sea People, the Tuatha de Danann, the Followers of the Goddess Danu. After his Irish conquest, he established the Lughnasadh, a fire ceremony celebrating a death-rebirth duality and associated with the winter solstice or the first fires of the New Year's Beltane ritual. It is still celebrated today as Lammas Day, or Lammastide, when bread baked from oven fires from the first wheat crop is consecrated in a special mass.[25]

In prehistoric America, the sacred temple-fire that was kept perpetually burning by a special attendant was known as the Loughe.[26] Lugh, its Old World derivation, seems certain, considering the ritual cremations which occurred in Aztalan and the orientation of its chief temple to the winter solstice. In view of the numerous native American traditions of ancestral beginnings after a Great Flood in the east, contrasted with the Irish deity's Atlantean grandfather, the Lughnasadh-Loughe fire ceremonies find a common denominator in Atlantis.

It has not been the purpose of these two chapters to present arguments for the geologic reality of Atlantis. However, to avoid all mention of its possible impact on our inquiry would have left a great gap in our understanding of America's ancient copper riddle, because the existence of Plato's island-civilization answers many important questions continually surfacing during our inquiry into the prehistory of Rock Lake.

Certainly, there is the very real danger of trying to solve one unknown by another. But the risk is worth taking if it brings us closer to the truth by illuminating parts of the picture otherwise hidden for lack of information. As far as our investigation up to this point is concerned, we are primarily interested in Atlantis insofar as it helps us to better envision that picture in its totality, to remove prehistoric Wisconsin from an isolated vacuum, if that is possible, and to demonstrate its connection to contemporary forces at work in the outside world. Only the reader may decide if such a broader objectivity assists him or her to visualize Rock Lake in the context of Bronze Age Europe and its oceanic medium—Atlantis.

·5·

The Rock Lake Mystery: A Worldwide Phenomenon

See the round towers of other days in the waves beneath them shining.
                    —*Irish folk song sung by fishermen in Lough Neagh*

A t the time of its publication, I considered *The Lost Pyramids of Rock Lake* the study of an absolutely unique archaeological enigma. Not long after its release, however, I was very surprised to learn of a virtually identical scenario occurring on the other side of the world. Thanks to a friend at the University of Wisconsin in Madison, a copy of my book was sent to Professor Nobuhiro Yoshida, Director of the Japan Petroglyph Society. He was equally astounded to learn about Rock Lake, because his group of investigators had been engaged in similar researches at Lake Biwa, in the Shiga Prefecture of central Honshu, not far from Kyoto. The subject of much poetry because of its calm beauty, Biwa-ko is today famous mostly as a tourist attraction. But in the country's prehistory, it was the main water route between the Sea of Japan and the Inland Sea. It was here that Dr. Yoshida and his divers found several cone-shaped stone pyramids only twenty feet down, not far from shore. The stone structures each stand about five feet high.

The Japanese counterpart to Rock Lake was not the only one I was to learn about, however. Under Lake Titicaca, high in the Bolivian

Andes, scuba divers discovered several stone ruins, including at least two pyramidal structures, again about twenty feet beneath the surface. Lake Titicaca is the site for one of the oldest civilizations in the Americas and among the most baffling, predating the Incas by at least two thousand years. The Incas nonetheless regarded the lake as their most sacred center, where Manco Capac, the founding father of Andean society, first arrived after a great flood destroyed his island kingdom in the distant ocean.

The natives have adapted to the remarkably thin air at the twelve-thousand-foot-plus altitudes over the course of generations, evolving barrel-like chests and blood cells better able to carry oxygen. But even these specialized locals are physically unable to withstand more than circumscribed peariods of physical stress. They certainly could not have produced the phenomenal labor necessary to raise the colossal structures at Tiahuanaco, the great stone city near Lake Titicaca, which sheltered a hundred thousand people in the ancient past. How they could have even lived in such a restrictive environment, let alone be burdened with the construction of a cyclopean metropolis, is beyond comprehension. The air is so thin in the altiplano, most grain will not grow, and vegetables cannot ripen there. Yet surrounding the vast ruins of Tihuanaco are the remnants of agricultural terraces that formerly sprouted with all manner of crops presently impossible to grow on the sterile plateau. What could account for the remains of a populous civilization in such an inhospitable land?

Vincent Gaddis, the author of *Native American Myths and Mysteries* (1991), offers a bold explanation:

> The most likely solution to the Tiahuanaco enigma is startling and runs counter to orthodox geological and archaeological theories. It is simply that the mountain had risen considerably after the city had been built. The conservative view is that mountain making is a slow, continuous process during hundreds of thousands of years. The idea that a large land mass can be raised thousands of feet in a short time, geologically speaking, is rejected. Tiahuanaco challenges this dogma. At some period in the past, the entire Titicaca plateau was at or below sea level with its lakes forming part of a sea gulf. At a later time, perhaps, a city was built and surrounded by farming terraces on the elevations around it. There was a final upheaval and the plateau was raised to its present height, making the city uninhabitable.[1]

Grand entrance to Tiahuanaco

A Harbor in the Sky

Radical as Gaddis' theory may be, it was lent credibility by Leonard Darwin, president of the Royal Geographical Society, together with Arthur Pozansky, regarded as "Bolivia's greatest savant."[2] Pozansky believed Tiahuanaco was built, not as the virtually uninhabitable mountain-city it is today, but as a seaport on the ocean. His conclusion is supported by the massive wall that famed oceanographer Jacques Cousteau attempted to photograph at the bottom of Lake Titicaca. The sunken rampart runs perfectly straight at right angles to the shore, pointing directly toward Tiahuanaco, as though it were part of a harbor facility or breakwater for the docking of large vessels. We recall the pre-Inca tradition of Manco Capac, who arrived at Titicaca from over the sea. In its present situation, the lake represents the least likely landfall after an ocean voyage.

Orogeny, or "mountain building," is understood by geologists as a very slow, natural process, involving many millions of years of virtually imperceptible movement. But that understanding was called into question as recently as the January 1994 earthquake that struck Los Angeles, California. Although registering 6.6 on the Richter scale, it was by no means a megaquake such as those that still occur in modern times throughout China, Turkey, and Armenia. Seismologists were astounded to observe that the Los Angeles earthquake actually pushed up sections of the San Gabriel Mountains almost two feet in about one minute! So, clearly, the sudden rise of the Andes, enough to raise them from sea level to more than twelve thousand feet in the space of a few thousand years, is entirely possible after all, given that same or greater seismic upheavals were at work in South America. In fact, that part of the world is one of the most seismically active areas on Earth.

Yet other evidence of a completely different kind likewise supports the original location of Tiahuanaco; namely, the discovery at that pre-Inca city of several anomalous strata of oyster shells, as cited on page 166 of Peter Tompkins' *Mysteries of the Mexican Pyramids* (Harper & Row, NY, 1976). It is difficult for us to imagine that the Andes Mountains did indeed rise twelve thousand feet into the sky, carrying a whole city with them, only because we really know so little about all the geologic potentialities of our own very dynamic planet. When I visited the High Andes in November 1994, I was surprised to find an abundance of unfossilized *seashells* among the ruins.

David Hatcher Childress, the American explorer who investigated Lake Titicaca in the late 1980s, described its sunken ruins this way in *Lost Cities & Ancient Mysteries of South America* (1986):

> Local Indians have reported observing buildings and roofs in the lake, and that after long droughts when the water level was low, they could even touch the tops of the buildings with their poles! This was written off as superstitious talk until the early 1970s, when an American dive team discovered what was literally a sunken city on the eastern shore of Lake Titicaca! Near Bolivia's Porto Acosta, in about 65 feet (20 m) of water can be found the ruins of an ancient city. There are reports of other sunken cities in Lake Titicaca, and it was these rumours that may have piqued Jacques Cousteau's interest.[3]

On pages 208 and 209, he reproduces actual photographs "of colossal structures on the bottom of Lake Titicaca."

Remarkably, when the Bolivian Indians touched the submerged ruins with their poles, they duplicated Lee Wilson's action when he touched the underwater pyramid in Rock Lake for the first time in 1900, with the tip of his oar. This parallel proves that the subsurface sites lie at similar depths. But Lake Titicaca's resemblance to Rock Lake extends even beyond the stone structures at the bottom of both bodies of water: The name "Titicaca" means "Rocky Puma Lake."

Bimini's Sunken "Road"

The most recently famous of these kindred sites is the so-called "Bimini Road" in the Bahamas due east of southern Florida. The underwater feature in question is what appears to be a gargantuan stone wall some three hundred feet long, off the northern shore of little Bimini Island. First discovered accidentally from the air in 1969, the structure comprises cut and fitted stones, many of massive proportions. Dismissed out of hand by establishment scholars as nothing more than an atypical formation of natural beach rock, core samples taken from the Road compared with local beach rock along the Bimini coast showed that the mineral composition of the two was unrelated.

In truth, the structure resembles the pre-Inca stonework of Sacsatiuaman in Peru and the pre-Roman remains of Lixus on the Atlantic shores of Morocco, lending credence to an Atlantean identity for the Bimini find. Neither a wall nor a road, its rounded terminus, the so-called "J-section," suggests it was originally part of a harbor facility, perhaps a breakwater.

In this, too, it has another provocative correspondent in Morocco. In the waters just outside Agadir, on the country's south Atlantic coast, lie the remains of a massive harbor, thought by some historians to be Phoenician, but already ancient when the Romans arrived in the late first century B.C. Aside from its general resemblance to the Bimini site, its location in Morocco may have long ago comprised the second kingdom of Atlantis. In Plato's account (the *Critias*), the name of its king was Gadeiros; *Agadir* appears to be an Arab rendering of the Atlantean name.

The Bimini structure bears additional resemblance to another South American ruin, this one in Bolivia and also underwater. It is the prehistoric harbor works at the bottom of Lake Titicaca, described above. No less remarkably, both it and the Bimini feature lie at generally the same depth, about twenty feet beneath the surface.

"Rock Lakes" in Europe

As my overseas research expanded, I learned that there are still other parts of the globe that feature ancient stone buildings under water, mostly lakes. Even Scotland's Loch Ness, better known for its elusive monster, conceals small stone ruins of circular structures (cairns) divers describe as miniature towers. These monuments, too, lie at relatively shallow depths, from twenty to thirty feet down.

An even more spectacular underwater find in Scotland was made during 1984, when archaeologists in scuba gear found the ruins of an entire town lying twelve feet beneath the surface of Loch Hess. They discovered the remains of domed, wooden structures built on stilts, accompanied by pyramidal piles of flat stones no different from those reported under Wisconsin's Rock Lake. An almost identical, although much larger, site was revealed during a sustained drought that drastically lowered water levels at Switzerland's Greifenwaldsee in 1898. Lake residents were baffled at the sight of acres of prehistoric support posts protruding from the exposed mud bottom. Greifenwaldsee's sunken village has been confidently dated to 4,200 years ago.

In Ireland, at a small lake, Lough Neagh, anyone venturing out on its waters could "see the round towers of other days in the waves beneath them shining." The words belong to an old folk song quoted by Giraldus Cambrensis, a scholar of the High Middle Ages, when the stone buildings, lying less than twenty feet below the surface, could be seen. Since then, Lough Neagh has silted up with agricultural run-off, totally obscuring the underwater anomalies. The same fate is in store for Rock Lake's pyramids for identical reasons. The Irish comparison with Rock Lake is striking, because, even though separated as they are by vast distances, both sites feature "round towers," even at the same depth.[4]

Other American Sunken Cities

Nor is Wisconsin the only state in the Union to have submerged pyramids. During a visit to Toltec Mounds Archaeological Park in Arkansas, I learned of a former site nearby that contained several prehistoric structures half sunk, others entirely submerged in a small lake not far from the Arkansas River. They were sketched in the late nineteenth century before a local dam project destroyed them. Illustrations of these structures appeared in an 1895 edition of Pope's *Early Days of Arkansas*. Remarkably, they bore a striking resemblance to the conical mounds under Rock Lake, suggesting both sites were products of a common culture.

Actually, the Arkansas mounds fit perfectly into our interpretation of prehistoric America. They were logically located along the primary river route taken by the ore-bearing freighters from the copper mines in the north and out into the Gulf of Mexico for the return voyage to Atlantis. If nothing else, the lake pyramids of Arkansas prove that claims for identical structures in Rock Lake are not based on fantasy, but find parallel material evidence elsewhere.

Just before I began writing *Atlantis in Wisconsin*, I was introduced to a man who told me of an outstanding underwater sighting he made exactly fifty years before. At that time, Herbert Sawinski was a World War II trainee in the U.S. Navy's Underwater Demolition Training program. Instruction dives were conducted in Wisconsin's Lake Geneva, only forty-three miles southeast of Rock Lake. Sawinski and his fellow classmates were engaged in the mock salvage of a ditched aircraft at the South Harbor area of the lake. They struggled across the muddy bottom in their canvas drysuits, with globular copper and glass helmets, weighted boots, and a confusion of air hoses and life lines. These were the days before scuba gear freed divers from the heavy, entangling restrictions of "hard-hat" subsurface exploration.

Thus engaged in their military classwork, they were distracted by the sudden appearance of a large, unusual building, an anomalous vision under thirty feet of water not far from the airplane on which they practiced their salvaging techniques. They examined the massive structure carefully in the clear visibility afforded by Lake Geneva's clean waters. It was built of round and flat stones all fitted together in a pyramidal arrangement resembling a gigantic tent. Both ends terminated in distinctly triangular configurations, and the sides sloped steeply to an apex that ran the length of the hundred-foot-long monument. It stood about twelve feet above the mud bottom, which was everywhere else devoid of stones.

In a letter, Sawinski wrote:

> The 'wall' appeared in about 25 to 30 feet of water and generally ran north and south, in other words, we crossed it while working east and west off the shoreline. At the time, I could not figure out what a wall would be doing here, unless someone had erected it on the ice for some reason and later, in the spring melts, it sank. However, the stones were not in a jumbled pile, but were carefully placed in what appeared to be a tapered wall.[5]

All the divers agreed that the structure was obviously manmade and wondered if it had been once part of some docking facility. It never occurred to them that it might belong to a prehistoric civilization. In any case, the ridge-top stone mound's location two hundred yards from shore defined it as something other than a dock. A few years after he war, Sawinski learned of a Wisconsin archaeologist who was quoted in the Milwaukee press to the effect that the subsurface anomaly was a genuine archaeological site that merited investigation. An underwater photograph that accompanied the article convinced Sawinski that it was the same stone mound he and his fellow divers had encountered during the war.

Apparently, more persons than those involved in the Navy's U.D.T. classes saw the structure; but, so far as I was able to determine, no further dives to study or relocate its exact position were subsequently undertaken.

When Sawinski and his comrades asked local residents about the sunken pyramid, they were further surprised to learn that generations of fishermen at nearby Lake Delavan, five miles northeast of Lake Geneva, claimed to have sometimes glimpsed a large "stone wall" beneath the keels of their boats. Sawinski's description of the structure he examined in 1942 matches exactly the large stone mound at the bottom of Rock Lake referred to in native American tradition as the Temple of the Moon and known to our investigators as the Limnatis Pyramid.

In 1993, John Wolford, at Western Michigan University (Kalamazoo), described a pyramidal stone structure in shallow depths at a small lake in western Massachusetts. A similar structure in his own state is so well known that the site is named after it: Walled Lake. Remarkably, both the Michigan and Massachusetts locations are on the same longitudinal line (34 degrees) with Rock Lake.[6]

Proof of a Worldwide Cataclysm?
Japan's Lake Biwa, Lake Titicaca high in the mountains of South America, the Bimini Road, Scotland's Loch Ness, the Irish Lough Neagh, Alabama's lake mounds, Wisconsin's Lake Geneva, Lake Delavan, and Rock Lake—I did not know what to make of the similar, sometimes identical, often pyramidal monuments they all shared in common. That many of them appear at least culturally related seems clear. But what factors could have been responsible for these relative finds in such widely scattered parts of the world?

Dr. Yoshida envisions some planet-wide change that sent the stone monuments to their watery graves:

The strange coincidences of ancient ruins at the bottom of lakes around the world suggests that the earth underwent some drastic change in its magnetic polarity after the fourth millennium B.C. Such a change may also explain the human migrations which took place on a world-wide scale during the same period. Mongolians migrated northward, while people in the Middle East left their fertile lands for northern Asia. They had to leave their homelands because it was no longer possible for them to continue living there. A massive climate change took place. The rich, green fields of North Africa turned to desert and the fertile lands of Central Asia were also threatened by hot conditions. As the earth changed its angle, there must have occurred a massive sinking of ground somewhere in the world, causing the ground-bases of Rock Lake, Lake Biwa, Loch Ness, etc. to shift enough to drown their stone monuments.[7]

David Childress elaborated on Dr. Yoshida's theory:

During a possible pole shift, created by a huge build-up of ice at both poles, the Pacific tectonic plate sank, and South America assumed the form we see today.

Hugh Auchincloss Brown, in his book *Cataclyms of the Earth* speculated that these pole shifts happen every seven to nine thousand years, depending on the build-up of ice at the poles. In fact, some navigation maps used as recently as the 1500s show Antarctica *ice free*! Today, 90% of all the fresh water on earth is estimated to be incased in the Antarctic ice mass, growing at a rate of 52 billion tons annually.

This does not take into account the loss of some ice to melting, creation of icebergs, etc. Even so, Brown cites a 1960 study that showed that the Antarctic ice mass increases its accumulation by 293 cubic miles annually. This is considerable, even in relationship to the total mass of the earth. Brown also shows that the South Pole's center of mass is approximately 350 miles off-center from the geographic South Pole, along the 80-degree East Meridian. According to one of the cataclysmic theories, the earth will flip like a top once it has been destabilized enough by the ice cap....

Could the sunken city near Porto Acosta actually be a city from the pre-cataclysmic times...?[8]

The sunken stone monuments scattered throughout the world could be clues to more than some archaeological mystery. Perhaps they are mute testimony to a natural catastrophe or planet-wide transformation that upset the earth's geologic balance and drowned man's early attempt at civilization. The deluged structures of four continents may have been inundated by the same forces that drastically shoved Tiahuanaco into the mountainous skies of Bolivia. What happened before may happen again, as Brown suggests. And as the popular historian Will Durant made clear: "Civilizations exist by geological consent, subject to change without notice."

•6•

What Do the Stone Mounds Conceal?

The entity was among those of the second generation of Atlanteans who struggled northward from Yucatan, settling in what is now a portion of Kentucky, Indiana, Ohio, being among those of the earlier period known as Mound Builders.
—*Edgar Cayce*

Critics of our finds beneath Rock Lake insisted we were mistaking natural formations, the residue of glaciers that retreated across Wisconsin twelve thousand years ago, for manmade monuments. But during a subsequent trip through Ohio, I visited an archaeological park known as Mound City for its numerous earthworks. Two of its features so resembled formations I had already observed under Rock Lake that I was convinced a common culture was responsible for the Wisconsin structures as well.

Mound City is an ancient necropolis similar to the City of the Dead at the bottom of Rock Lake, comprising some twelve square acres adjacent to the Scioto River. The site has been classified as Hopewellian, an entirely academic term archaeologists use to place its otherwise unidentified creators within a coherent scheme for American prehistory. But the real identity of the Mound City inhabitants is unknown.

They prospered from the first through the fifth centuries A.D., when, for obscure reasons, they abruptly abandoned the ceremonial center. While its sudden demise seems fairly certain, its real beginnings are far from sure, and the Ohio necropolis may have origins far deeper into the past than the experts are willing to acknowledge. The early users of the sacred precinct dwelt in river villages and only visited Mound City on religious occasions. These included ancestor worship, judging from the select individuals, all male—political leaders and shamans—interred in the earthworks. It was not a public cemetery, but a spiritually powerful reserve for ritual and psychic empowerment, where only the most important dead were permitted burial.

Described as "more gracile" in the local museum literature, the Mound Builders were physically different from the Plains Indians, who occupied the vicinity centuries after the site was forsaken. The entombments were as fabulous as they were bizarre. In one pyramidal mound, two skeletons were stretched out in a chamber, its floor covered with huge, delicate flakes of pale-white mica imported from New England shores. Another earthwork entombed a corpse surrounded by more than three hundred stone effigy pipes superbly crafted to represent frogs, deer, bears, serpents, and other animal symbols of the soul's rebirth.

But it was the exterior shapes of the Ohio mounds that most impressed me for their resemblance to parallel examples spied in the depths of Rock Lake. At the center of the ceremonial plaza is a ridge-top temple mound that could pass for the double of a sunken structure discovered by master diver Doug Gossage in the southeast quadrant of the lake in 1988, save only that the Ohio counterpart was made of earth instead of stone.

The Volcano Mound

Even more remarkably similar is a dome-shaped feature that originally resembled a volcano, its "crater" since filled in with debris and reconfigured by erosional forces. But in its intended condition, the opening at the top was filled with many thousands of white marine shells. I have personally encountered two examples under Rock Lake exactly the same as the Mound City structures, save again that they were constructed of stone instead of soil. For size, shape, and the crater filled with white marine shells, they are identical. Anyone who would like to see just what some of the lost pyramids of Rock Lake really look like on dry land need only visit Ohio's Mound City.

That the ancient inhabitants of Rock Lake/Aztalan and Mound City were at least cut from the same cultural cloth, if they were not the same people, is borne out by the numerous civilized comparisons they shared. Both worked skillfully in large quantities of copper; they even shared much of the same trading network, and cremation practices were identical at either site. Mound City may have been an outpost of the Aztalaners ruling from Wisconsin, where they controlled the copper trade.

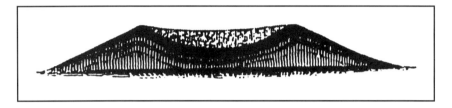

Burial mound at Ohio's Mound City. It identically resembles structures found in Rock Lake, even to the thousands of white stones filling its summit.

But perhaps the most convincing parallel evidence that authenticates the colossal structures lying at the bottom of Rock Lake are (or were!) the numerous stone mounds that once dotted the Midwestern landscape. Unknown to even many professional archaeologists today, these manmade, elongated pyramids were huge sepulchers which matched the underwater features of Wisconsin detail for detail. Skeptics of so-called "pyramids" in Rock Lake have long pointed out that native Americans did not work in stone on a large scale, that all their mounds were made of soil and clay only. The structures seen by divers were obviously glacial debris that just happened to resemble artificial handiwork. Nature was imitating art, that was all.

But in the summer of 1992, I was contacted by John Wolford of Milford, Michigan. He sent me a video shot that year of an unusual mound in a place called Heritage Park, a 212-acre preserve just south of the Shiawassee River. The river connects directly into Lake Michigan through Saginaw Bay and beyond to the copper mining regions of the Upper Peninsula. The Heritage Park mound is about ten feet tall, a hundred feet long, perhaps fifteen feet in diameter, oriented due north, and made of piled and fitted stones; in other words, a duplicate on dry land of the structures encountered sixty feet below Rock Lake.

Wolford's find is perhaps the last of an unknown number of similar mounds, most of which were dismantled by farmers. Fortunately, at least a few were properly surveyed and excavated before their destruction, and the evidence they contained confirmed not only their manmade origins. They throw new light on their drowned counterparts in Rock Lake. Among the most convincing parallel proof used to exist at two sites along the water routes from the Atlantic Ocean to the copper mining regions, appropriately enough. Ontario's Massassaga Mound and the Perch Lake Mound in upper New York state were duplicates of the volcano-like monuments examined by divers under Rock Lake.

The first modern excavation of one of the puzzling structures took place as late as 1956, near the town of St. Paul, in the central southeast section of Indiana on the Flatbush River. Known as the C.L. Lewis Stone Mound, it was in immediate danger of being removed by the owner of the private property on which it was found when field researchers from the Indiana Historical Society were allowed to examine it for any possible archaeological significance. Like the sunken pyramids, it was generally regarded as a kame, or glacial remnant. In the words of James H. Kellar, who supervised the dig, "The first hour of excavation settled any doubt there may have been regarding the origin of the stone pile."[1]

Excavation

Inside, he and his assistants found fourteen separate human burials, with an additional twenty-two persons who had been cremated. They lay in a shallow, ring-like ditch, over which the stones had been piled into a pyramidal shape.

The burials themselves obviously belonged to persons of prominence, judging from the special care that went into their entombment. A beautifully woven grass mat had been placed over the bodies, which were laid out in an east-west orientation. A veritable trove of copper items had been offered to the dead, including twenty-six finely crafted beads, four bracelets, and a single ring. There were mother-of-pearl ornamental beads, an impressive stone gorget (a badge of high political authority that was suspended around the neck), and a magnificent dagger. As Kellar marveled, "The large blade exhibits exceptionally fine workmanship. The material is light pink in color and is unlike any of the cherts or chalcedonies from any of the better known aboriginal quarries."[2]

The cremated burials were not intruded after the structure had been made. "Without question, cremation of human remains had taken place in situ."[3] The bodies themselves represented a mysterious collection. "The remains were covered with an extremely heavy deposit of red ochre."[4] The same funeral practice was employed by the Guanches, the ancient inhabitants of the Canary Islands we have identified with the Atlantean seafarers and copper miners of the Upper Peninsula. Some of the stone mound's corpses had been stripped of flesh previous to burial, and one skull showed that its owner in life had received the attention of a prehistoric dentist: "A small copper object was found which was originally associated with an upper incisor, fitted over the bottom to form a sheath-like covering."[5] There was a line of seven skulls next to the skeleton of a headless man, and the excavators puzzled over a nearby diorite chisel.

This too, like the other artifacts, pointed "without exception to an Adena relationship," just as "the gorget is the diagnostic Adena form."[6] "Adena" is the modern archaeological expression for a generalized culture centered in southern Ohio, from which it spread out to neighboring states before 1000 B.C.[7] The Adena lived in circular houses with roofs resembling cone-shaped pyramids. They also built "rock shelters" (a term for the ruinous condition of ancient stone structures) and traded extensively for copper and shell. This "Adena" period not only identifies the time parameters for the Lewis Stone Mound, but coincides with the occupation date for Rock Lake's Lymnatis Pyramid, which bears so close a resemblance to the Indiana mound. But comparison between the two sites by no means ends with their common origins in the second millennium B.C.

In the Indiana tomb, we find the same skull cult of the headless man found in Rock Lake's decapitated-effigy mound and in Aztalan's headless-man grave, the earthwork shaped into a man without a head and the twin skulls placed at the very center of the ceremonial enclosure. These two skulls, especially because of their position at the midpoint of Aztalan, defined the ancient city as a center for the skull cult that flourished at least as far as Ohio's Mound City, described above. There, shaman masks made from human skulls were discovered, appropriately enough, in a mound at the very center of the precinct.

The diorite "chisel" removed from the Lewis structure was actually a miner's tool of the kind used by the Aztalaners to work the copper of Michigan's Upper Peninsula, an identification made all the clearer by the profusion of copper artifacts accompanying the stone mound burials. Meanwhile, the man with a copper cap on his front tooth was the beneficiary of dentistry, a civilized trait of the distant Aztalaners. Interestingly, the Adena culture, which appears to have linked southern Wisconsin to Indiana around the twelfth century B.C., is known by its conical pyramids, the same unusual features seen beneath Rock Lake.

The bodies laid out with respect in the Lewis structure were aligned east-west, an orientation suggesting the numerous solar fixes recurring throughout Aztalan and Rock Lake, where the Turtle and Headless Man effigy mounds are oriented toward sunset. Those cremations that took place prior to the construction of the St. Paul mound reflect identical practices, as revealed in the earthworks that once lined the shores of Rock Lake and at Aztalan's Pyramid of the Moon, where ten bodies were cremated. Probably the finds made in the Lewis mound are very similar to the grave goods and inhumations which still repose undisturbed in the great, sunken necropolis.

In any case, it seems clear that the Indiana mound was raised by the same culture bearers responsible for Wisconsin's underwater sepulchers. Its mirror-like resemblance to the Limnatis Pyramid not only defines the Rock Lake find as a genuine manmade monument, it demonstrates that the Wisconsin stone mound is not an archaeological anomaly, but part of a cultural pattern extending throughout the Midwest long before the arrival of so-called "Mound Builders" of the Mississippian Tradition.

The Rock Lake Parallel
Similar to the controversy still going on over the supposedly Ice Age origins of the Rock Lake formations, the Lewis mound was first thought to have been only so much rocky debris dumped by retreating glaciers, until archaeologists excavated its interior. The same desecration would very likely have to take place before establishment skeptics could be satisfied that Rock Lake conceals something more than Ice Age flotsam.

Of the several dozen stone mounds known to have existed in the Midwest, all of them were located in close proximity to water, often rivers, but sometimes lakes. And they were usually colossal structures, similar in size to the hundred-foot long Limnatis Pyramid of Rock Lake. The Edwards Stone Mound #1, found in Hamilton County, Ohio, on the banks of the Little Miami River, was 120 feet long, nine feet high, and a hundred feet wide. Precisely like the Rock Lake struc-

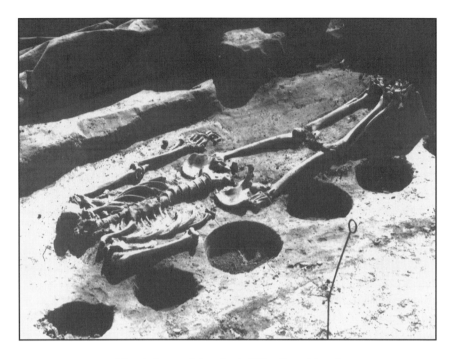

The skeleton of Aztalan's "Headless Giant"

ture discovered in 1967 by scuba diver Jack Kennedy, after whom the monument was named, it was composed of stones from a riverbed. Its contents of deer leg bones in company with human burials is reminiscent of the five deer leg bones recovered by divers from Rock Lake's underwater structures between 1970 and 1990.

The Edwards Mound also contained the grave of a child covered by a turtle shell, a startling parallel to the pair of boys buried in Aztalan under a carapace from the Gulf of Mexico, funeral practices encountered nowhere else.

"The floor of the mound on the south side was burned to a depth of 2 to 3 inches over an area 10 by 12 feet," Kellar reported, the same kind of ritual cremation that occurred at Rock Lake/Aztalan.[8] While other peoples have either cremated their dead or interred them, only the ancient Wisconsinites and their fellow culture bearers in other Midwestern states combined both cremation and inhumation within the same tomb. A dog was also buried with obvious care and respect inside the Edwards Mound, and we recall the dog's cult status among the

Aztalaners. Most telling of all was Edwards Mound's headless man, evidence of the skull cult known from Rock Lake to Indiana and again identifying the stone monuments with a particular mystery religion.

A stone mound once stood at Fort Ancient, an enormous wall entirely encircling the top of a high hill in the Ohio Valley north of Cincinnati. The mound's appearance preceded this sacred enclosure, an indication that the stone mound culture could antedate the Adena time frame by at least several centuries, pushing stone mound construction back to the thirteenth century B.C. and before, to the years when Michigan's copper deposits were being furiously worked by the Atlantean miners.[9]

The Fort Ancient stone mound had some surprises of its own. "Also, an unusual boatstone was recovered. It was made of red sandstone, drilled and had a truncated cone projecting from the side opposite the groove."[10] While the "truncated cone" belongs to conical configurations sacred to Rock Lake's mortuary architecture, a red ceremonial stone, hixtonite, was found embedded in an underwater structure during exploratory dives in September 1991. Here, too, the skull cult made its reappearance. "Two isolated human skulls had been placed southeast of the central burial area."[11]

The Prehistoric Tower
Ohio could also boast the tallest known stone mound, in Licking County, site of the immense and equally ancient Newark Earthworks, the largest astronomical observatory in the world. Known naturally enough as the Great Stone Mound, it stood more than fifty feet high, the considerable achievement of a vanished people. Curiously, many of the monuments were, like the Great Stone Mound, in the company of geoglyphs. Ohio's Tarlton Cross and the Alligator effigy (which shared the same county as the Newark colossus) were guarded by stone mounds.

Not surprisingly, their greatest concentration occurred in Wisconsin. There were six or seven around Lake Winnebago and at Butte de Morts, whose name, "the Hills of the Dead," is an obvious memory of the massive burial mounds that formerly occupied the area until the early nineteenth century.

The Lake Winnebago stone monuments stood astride the water route from Rock Lake to Copper Culture State Park, an old way-station between southern Wisconsin and the Upper Peninsula copper mines. Other stone mounds were similarly and appropriately grouped around the ancient former shorelines of Rock Lake. One at Chippewa Falls stood not far from Rice Lake and Pipestone Mountain, whence the Aztalaners made pilgrimage to obtain the sacred mineral, catlinite, for their ceremonial pipes.

A lone example could be found at Hixton, source of another ritual mineral, the glowing-red hixtonite, which has been seen among the stone cairns of Rock Lake. Cairns, or little circular towers used for arcane ritual purposes, are today found almost exclusively under its waters, but they were once common landmarks across the prairie states, according to Kellar.[12] A few are known to Upper Great Lakes tribes as Pokasawa pits. They resemble firebreaks, but the tribal elders still refuse to reveal their real esoteric function.

It is clear, then, that the stone mounds, conical pyramids, and cairns silently reposing in the emerald gloom of Rock Lake were long ago part of an Adena, or, more likely, a pre-Adena culture that spread far beyond its headquarters in southern Wisconsin. Contrary to the statements of many critics, the ancient Americans did indeed work with stone on a large scale. Moreover, examples like Indiana's C.L. Lewis mound are virtually identical to Rock Lake's subsurface structures, a correspondence that demonstrates their definition as man-made monuments. In learning about the massive stone features that once adorned the heartland of our country, we may begin to visualize the unsuspected magnificent civilization that once rose to prominence in America at a time when pharaohs ruled Imperial Egypt.

.7.

New Revelations,
New Enigmas

The past is in its grave, 'though its ghost haunts us.
—Robert Browning

Readers of *The Lost Pyramids of Rock Lake* will recall a chapter describing the legend of a "monster" associated with its depths. First reported in the mid-nineteenth century, sightings of the Loch Ness type beast continued into the early 1920s. Remembered as dark brown in color, with a thick, serpentine torso sprouting a long neck and a horse-like head, it entered local history as "Rocky," although resident Winnebago Indians regarded the phenomenon more seriously. They reminded skeptics of the gigantic effigy mound portraying a water creature that lay along the southern shore of Rock Lake since prehistoric times, until its obliteration to make way for a railway trestle after the turn of the last century. They still insist that a spirit guardian, a kind of thought-form placed in the lake to protect the ancient sunken tombs of holy men, continues to prowl its depths.

It was not long after *The Lost Pyramids of Rock Lake* was released that I received a phone call from a man who had seen the monster more recently. Joseph Davis is a retired business executive now residing near Galveston Bay, Texas. He founded and ran Finders, Inc., which located and supplied props for movie and theater companies.

75

But he is originally from Lake Mills, where his family owned a house near the lake. He never got a glimpse of the stone monuments beneath its surface, for all his free-diving attempts, but he knew about the controversial structures at an early age.

When just a boy in the 1930s, a German maid who lived on the opposite shore of Rock Lake and worked at his family home told of a strange image she saw beneath its surface. Her encounter took place on a sunny afternoon in late winter, when the lake was frozen over. As she crossed it on foot, she noticed that the waters just below the translucent ice cap were crystal clear. She could see straight to the bottom. Less than halfway out, she stopped in her tracks at the sight of a large, circular building down under the lake. The maid described it as resembling "an amphitheater."

Sixty years later, scuba divers would rediscover the same structure during the taping of an episode for NBC's popular television series, *Unsolved Mysteries*. At least twenty feet tall and perhaps fifty feet in diameter (precise dimensions were impossible to obtain because of obscuring silt), the volcano-shaped monument is what archaeologists know as an annular mound, a family crypt, in the walls of which were interred the remains of relatives; the conical depression at the top allowed for surviving family members to commune with the departed through a vision quest. Not long after, in 1937, Joe saw Max Nohl use a device to hunt the sunken pyramids. It was the premiere dive of the world's first self-contained underwater breathing apparatus (SCUBA, for short), and the lad was an eyewitness to history.

The Return of Rocky
Six summers later, Joe was a fifteen year old whose favorite pastime was scooting across the lake in his outboard-motor boat. But one hot afternoon in July 1943 remains forever fresh in his memory for its horror. He had sped out to a quiet area of Rock Lake, near its center and the so-called drop-off, a peculiar formation that rose steeply, then descended sharply to the bottom. He knew the fishing would be good here. As he readied his line, he was distracted by a disturbance in the water close to his boat. There was a billowing effect on the surface, perhaps ten or more feet across, as though something large was rising rapidly from below. He stared at it in surprise, the disturbance becoming more pronounced. Now he could make out some large, dark, indefinite shape moving upward through the water. The next moment, it broke the surface; first the back, then the torso of a living

beast. It was massive—a bulky six or seven feet in length. No doubt, it was alive, a brownish-black animal that seemed about to raise its neck or head when it suddenly slipped beneath the water, leaving an agitated surface in its wake.

The entire sighting lasted no more than a minute, but it was more than enough time for Joe to get a good, close look at the creature. Close to panic, he gunned his outboard and raced for shore. Emotionally shaken, he swore never to return to the lake and to keep the experience to himself. But his parents, aware of the change in their son, finally coaxed the story out of him. As he expected, they could not believe him. He must have been mistaken, they told him. What he had seen was only a log or a clump of lake weed. But Joe Davis knew what he saw, and with the retrospect of years, he is as sure now as he was then that there is indeed a sizable, unknown beast in Rock Lake.

His encounter is the most recent sighting known to have taken place. There may have been others since then, but no eyewitnesses have come forth, perhaps for fear of ridicule.

David Hatcher Childress, President of the World Explorers Club, wonders if the lake does indeed harbor an animal with a very low metabolic rate that allows it to survive in the deepest section, which is noted for its extremely low year-round temperatures. Perhaps, when the lake was formed by a retreating glacier at least twelve thousand years ago, a family of now otherwise extinct creatures settled there. The very habitation of the lake by these beasts may have rendered that body of water extraordinarily sacred to the first humans who discovered it. To them, the presence of such creatures was proof of its special, hallowed character.

So the lake became a holy burial ground, protected by its resident water-guardian. In other words, it was the existence of this beast that was responsible for transforming the lake into a sacred City of the Dead. Somehow, at least a few of the animals (either mammals or reptiles; who knows?) survived into the present, but are only very infrequently seen, because they spend virtually all their lives in the deepest, darkest, coldest, most forbidding fathoms of the lake.

While no other diver has ever witnessed the Wisconsin lake monster, virtually all of them told me they have at one time or another experienced feelings of alarm under Rock Lake related to the uncanny sensation that they are being watched or even stalked. Skeptics may scoff at divers' tales, but it is nonetheless a fact that one's instinctual acuity is substantially heightened under water, if only because the difference between life and death is obvious and ever present in a sub-surface environment.

Mysteries of a less threatening kind abound throughout southern Wisconsin.

Token of Ancient Visitors

In 1984, Wayne May, Rock Lake's indefatigable investigator and elo-quent spokesman for our efforts, found a curious object while explor-ing the banks of the Crawfish River in Aztalan. Only about 1¼ inches long and ¾ of an inch across, the walnut-like article is self-evidently manmade. Already broken into eight separate pieces before its dis-covery, its interior was solid but did not serve to explain the artifact's identity. It resembled a child's spinning top, although it could also pass for a fishnet weight or plumb bob used in surveying. Spectro-analysis could not define the object, but test results at the University of Wisconsin's geology department (Eau Claire) in 1993 were nonethe-less startling. They revealed that the artifact was made of fossilized bone. The analysis was unable to determine if it had been carved before or after its fossilization. If before, then its manufacture must be unthinkably old.

The object seemed beyond definition, until Wayne, in the course of his endless research, was surprised to find it illustrated in a copy of *New Treasures of the Past* by Brian Fagan (London, 1987). There, on page 75, was a photograph of the object he had discovered in Aztalan, or at any rate a clay version that was a dead ringer for it. But the item por-trayed in Fagan's book did not come from Wisconsin. It was found among a cache of related artifacts during an archaeological dig at Tello in Mesopotamia.

Actually, dozens of similar finds are scattered throughout several museums in Europe and the United States. All about the same size, they came in different shapes. Some were wedges or discs incised with curious lines or regularly perforated. Others were cones, triangles, and rectangles. For years, the purpose of these small objects was unknown. In 1969, however, University of Texas archaeologist Denise Schmandt-Besserat positively identified them as tokens used in commercial deal-ings. Each one stood for a single commodity, such as food, metal, timber, etc. When merchants traveled to do business with their clients in the ancient world, buyers were given tokens that were redeemable for goods purchased. The tokens were found all through Egypt, into Sumer, Syria, and Lebanon.

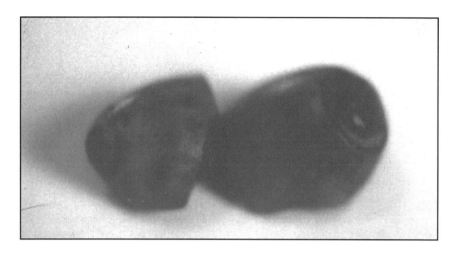

Nut-like object cracked in two.

Fagan writes, "The first major changes in the token system came between 3500 B.C. and 3100 B.C., when the first cities were appearing in Mesopotamia. Schmandt-Besserat believes that these changes came about in response to new complexities, both in the production of artifacts such as metal tools and in trade itself."[1] The trade in metal tools she emphasized coincides with the massive copper mining that was at that time just commencing at Michigan's Upper Peninsula. The Wisconsin object's identification as a trade token is underscored by the site of its discovery, along the banks of the Crawfish River in Aztalan, center of the North American copper trade.

According to Schmandt-Besserat, Wayne's find is a token signifying a single jar of oil. It also represents material evidence of ancient Near Eastern—i.e., Atlantean—visitors in prehistoric America, who did business up and down its central river systems.

Dogs of Rock Lake
No larger but no less intriguing than the petrified token was the tiny gilt statuette of a dog found atop a previously unnoticed Indian mound in Tyranena Park, a wooded area on the north shore of Rock Lake. The dog, as discussed in my previous volume, was venerated as a sacred animal by the ancient Aztalaners, while the statuette's manufacture in copper alloy fits in so well with Aztalan's significance as a copper-mining town. The dog was similarly the cult-figure of the

Canari, or Guanches, the original inhabitants of the Canary Islands, whose unmistakable connection with Aztalan was traced in *The Lost Pyramids of Rock Lake.*

The dog-theme connects Aztalan with more than the Canary Islands in the Atlantic, however. The ancient Greek poet, Homer, said that the main entrance to the palace of Atlantis was guarded on either side by the life-size statues of dogs. One was gold, the other of silver, probably signifying the sun and moon, respectively. Thus the dog as a religious symbol links Rock Lake and Aztalan to the metal-working Atlanteans, who came to Upper Michigan and Wisconsin in their quest for copper.

Given the spiritual regard with which dogs were held by the prehistoric Wisconsinites, the little figure resembles a cult object, an identity enforced by its fortuitous discovery atop what may be the last surviving above-water mound of Rock Lake. Apparent filing marks on the statuette have cast some doubt on its authenticity, but whether these were made at the time of its creation or long after has not yet been determined. Moreover, the style of its execution is highly reminiscent of the earth effigy mounds that once surrounded Aztalan's walls and the the shores of the lake.

The Dagger

Yet another fascinating little discovery was made in an obscure, rarely traveled area near the Red Cedar River, connected to the Rock Lake area via the Rock and Crawfish Rivers, several hundred miles to the southeast. This find is a four-inch long metal sheath containing a smaller blade of the same whitish-bronze metal. It is perhaps composed of copper with a strong tin base. Some perishable material that once wrapped around the pommel has rotted away. Provision for a clip is on the obverse of the sheath, which could have been attached to a belt. The blade's size defines it as a cultish item, since it seems too small for utilitarian purposes. Its age is impossible to gauge, but the delicacy of its workmanship bears no resemblance to the larger, cruder, pure copper blades annealed (or cold-hammered) by Plains Indians.

In fact, the Red Cedar knife appears to have been forged over intense heat, a technique not used by native Americans, but common among Bronze Age Europeans. Indeed, its tin-copper combination bespeaks the metalsmiths of the Old World in pre-Classical times. That resemblance is drawn still closer by the shape of the sheath and particularly the bip or knob at its point. It is a style that appeared prac-

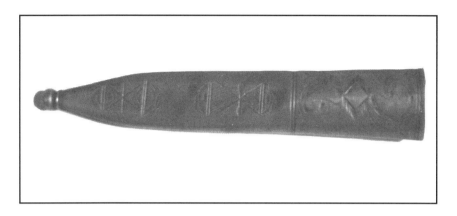

The engimatic metal sheath found near the Red Cedar River.
from The Ancient American, *Sept./Oct. 1993*

tically as a trademark throughout the ancient Western world, from Ireland and Spain to Italy and Asia Minor. Most intriguing of all perhaps are the enigmatic figures etched so gracefully on the sheath. They resemble nothing among the tribal cultures of Wisconsin's Plains Indians, suggesting instead early Bronze Age petroglyphs found along the Atlantic shores of continental Europe, in the British Isles and, appropriately enough, in the Canary Islands.

If the little dagger and its sheath are the results of neither native Americans nor some modern agency, then they appear to have belonged to a Bronze Age visitor from across the Atlantic, one among the thousands engaged in mining the Upper Peninsula. In fact, the Red Cedar represented a major water route to Michigan's copper sources, so the artifact's discovery on its banks certainly lies within the context of our argument. Also in the Red Cedar, about five miles from Colfax, is a nameless little island dangerous to reach because of the ever-turbulent waters that flow around it even in winter. At the center of the island is a large manmade mound. Actually, several other islets in the Red Cedar feature similar burial mounds virtually unknown to the outside world. One example is thirty feet high.

The Devil's Well
But the site near Colfax is extraordinary for a manmade well adjacent to the earthwork. The very obscure location of the island assures the ancient provenance of these two features. Known locally as the

"Devil's Well," it is oval shaped—three feet by ten feet—and is said to be bottomless. A fifty-foot rope weighted with a stone was lowered into it without hitting bottom. Water of outstanding clarity fills the Devil's Well, but, even under ideal light conditions, no one has been able to see its absolute depth.

Before Yuletide 1990, a startling find was made, not under Rock Lake, but near its southeastern shore, in the immediate vicinity of numerous effigy mounds that proliferated throughout the area prior to their modern destruction. A Lake Mills resident and member of the Ancient Earthworks Society discovered a three-foot-tall rock incised with deliberate markings resembling an inscription of some kind. A professional archaeologist was summoned. He said at first sight that the markings were obviously made by human agency and opined that they seemed to be letters from an Old English alphabet. When he was respectfully reminded that the Lake Mills area had been settled by German, not English immigrants, he changed his mind and dismissed the markings as scratches caused by a farmer's plow.

Aside from the swampy location at which the rock was found, an area impossible to farm, the lay discoverers were reluctant to embrace the official's hasty verdict because they were reminded of a similarly marked stone found during the 1920s in the Rock Lake vicinity. It, too, was first noticed by amateurs, then officially condemned as nothing more than plow scratches by salaried experts—until a visiting English archaeologist was so impressed with the apparent authenticity of the etched characters that he purchased the stone from its farmer-discoverer and took it back to London. Today, it is on display in the North American antiquities section of the British Museum, where it is cataloged as "the Jefferson County Stone (Wisconsin, U.S.A.) bearing a crypto-runic inscription."

The 1990 finders did not wish to let its companion piece be similarly lost through official indifference, so they sent photographs of the stone to the Epigraphic Society (California). Examiners there were unable to effect a decipherment of the supposed inscription. Nor could they determine if the markings even belonged to a script of any kind. All they were able to determine was that the etchings were indeed artificially made, not by the random action of a plow, but with deliberate purpose.

After the incised markings were chalked in, they less resembled writing than the elements of a drawing or map. The general consensus of those who have studied the stone in person tends toward this interpretation. If it is a map, then it bears a striking similarity to the

The Rock Lake Map-Stone

very place where the stone itself was found, near the eastern shore of
Rock Lake. More remarkable still, the "map" appears to show a pyramid in the lake at the same general position as a monumental structure discovered during our subsurface investigations.

What might be a road indicated by the lithic map leads from shore
out across the lake to the pyramid. Why would anyone need such a
map makes little sense, until we recall the Winnebago story of the
"foreign shamans" who allegedly deceived the common people by
pretending to walk on the water as they carried torches. They actually passed over a secret causeway just beneath the surface. It would
be important to know the precise location of such a causeway, which
might lead directly to one of the submerged monuments. Was the map
incised on the rock face as a mnemonic device traced by the fingers of
the shaman to reassure himself just previous to his water-walking act?

Map of the Pyramid?

Its other markings are open to provocative interpretations. Below, to the
right of center, a bird-like figure appears to be flying toward the "pyramid" in the lake. Some one hundred miles northwest of Rock Lake, a
bird-shaped effigy mound, near the shore, was built to seem as if it were
flying toward Devil's Lake, outside Baraboo. The bird was a common
image throughout native America as the shaman's own symbol of
higher transformation, astral projection, out-of-body experiences, levitation, and other feats of magic involving "flight" of some kind.

At the bottom of the puzzling stone is a trident, a particularly
revealing sign, because it was the emblem of the ancient Sea Peoples,
the Atlantean culture bearers, who spread civilization across the
Mediterranean world in the fourth millennium B.C. The trident was
also associated with Poseidon, the sea god, who, according to Plato's
account, was the foremost deity worshiped in Atlantis as its creator.
Finding this most identifiably Atlantean symbol on a suspicious
stone near the shores of Rock Lake coincides with all the numerous
scraps of evidence which, together, are forming a picture of ancient
Wisconsin as the Bronze Age clearing-house of prehistoric America.

Acceptance of this stone as a cartogram is lent credibility by the
finds of similar "rock maps" discovered in Michigan's copper mining
region. One was found on Beaver Island, in upper Lake Michigan, an
archaeologically rich site. Here monolithic observatories and sophisticated garden beds have been excavated. The Beaver Island petroglyph strongly resembles the configuration of lower Michigan itself.

While such an interpretation of its apparent diagram may at first seem fanciful, skeptics may be interested to learn that another rock map of Michigan's lower peninsula was found on the Lake Huron shore opposite Drummond Island. Still another representation of Michigan was retrieved in 1989 from the waters off Keweenaw Peninsula, focus of the ancient copper miners' most intensive operations, 5,300 years ago. The map is, in fact, shaped from a rectangular four-ton copper nugget ten feet long, four feet wide, and twenty inches thick. Underscoring its supposed function as a map is the specimen's smoothed surface and its obvious resemblance to the very place in which it was found. This copper billboard appears to have fallen overboard during transport between 3000 B.C. and 1200 B.C., when mining flourished along the Keweenaw Peninsula.[2] Given these comparative examples from Michigan, the Rock Lake stone's identity as a cartogram, possibly of the lake itself, seems likely.

Aztalan's Zemi Stone

I learned of another curious stone, this one from Aztalan itself, while visiting the mound site in September 1994. A friend from China and I were sitting atop the Pyramid of the Moon when we were approached by a fellow visitor, Ron Gordon, a resident of the modern town also known as Aztalan. Seeing Xue Ying from the back, with her long, raven hair and the brown dress she wore at the time, he assumed she was a native American until they were introduced. He said he was always interested in meeting with tribal Indians, because of a peculiar artifact he had found about fifteen years ago; maybe they could tell him something about it.

Perhaps a fifth of a mile southwest of Aztalan's archaeological zone, Ron was hunting for arrowheads in a densely overgrown area when he came upon a small hill. Perched at its summit was a strange-looking stone. Nearly three feet long, some eight inches at its widest base point and two feet high, it resembled the dorsal fin of a shark. There were no other rocks in the vicinity, and its position atop the hill bespoke some definite purpose. On closer inspection, it appeared to have been expertly carved from a kind of white granite; the sculpture, almost modernistic in the simplicity and linear clarity of its form, rose in a smooth, triangular shape from the base of the stone to a delicately thin apex. As a work of art, it had immediate appeal. But it certainly implied something else beside its aesthetic qualities.

One of the Greenwood mounds. Eight hundred years ago, a tall pole rising from its summit was used by Aztalan astronomers to predict the positions of certain stars.

It reminded me almost at once of a gnomon, a pointed object that casts the shadow of the sun to mark the passing hours of the day. Given its close proximity to Aztalan's Pyramid of the Sun, with its numerous solar orientations, Gordon's find must have originally played some part in relation to the astronomical observations constantly made from the ceremonial center nine centuries ago. Maybe, after all, it was not a sundial, but an alignment marker, such as the high posts which once stood tall against the western horizon from their mounds in the so-called Greenwood Group; they were used by ancient astronomers standing atop Aztalan's temple mounds to chart the positions of various celestial phenomena for their sacred calendar. Perhaps the gracefully fashioned stone served a similar purpose.

Most remarkable of all (but in keeping with our examination of Atlantean influences in Wisconsin), the stone sculpture Ron found, while unique in America's Midwest, is virtually identical to many dozens of so-called "Zemis" or "thunder stones" found in the Antilles. Actually, their distribution is confined to Puerto Rico and the eastern extremity of Santo Domingo. They appear to be cult objects, but archaeologists do not

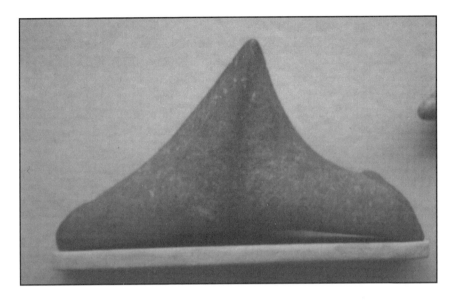

Zemi stone from Puerto Rico. Its resemblance to a
stone sculpture found near Aztalan is remarkable.
Museum of the American Indian, New York

have a clue as to their real functions nor to the identity of their creators, because they predate the Arawak inhabitants of the islands by many centuries. Lewis Spence, the greatest Atlantis scholar of the early twentieth century, suspected the Zemis' Atlantean connection in his monumental book, *The History of Atlantis* (London: University Books, 1926). He wrote (page 236), "They certainly seem to me to symbolize a deity, whose duty it was to uphold the earth, but who, like Atlas (the eponymous deity of Atlantis), occasionally felt the immensity of his burden and cast it from him, causing universal destruction and catastrophe."

Indeed, the Zemis appear to represent a volcanic island, some sacred mountain cone. Spence backs up his conclusion by citing various flood legends among the Macusi tribe of the Arawak and the Caribs. If the Wisconsin example is not itself a direct link with Atlantis, it or the notion behind it may have come from the Antilles, where we know the Aztalaners had commercial ties. In any case, finding such a stone in the immediate vicinity of their ceremonial center may have potentially astounding implications.

After Ron narrated the story of his discovery, he showed us the stone itself, which he happened to be carrying in the trunk of his car.

Xue Ying and I both thought it odd that he should be traveling around with this singular object. But we soon learned that he was deeply, inexplicably attached to his find and had, in fact, declined without hesitation several generous offers from collectors who wanted to purchase it. He likes to be near the stone as often as possible, as though to savor some significant connection he feels but cannot entirely understand. He is one of many persons who have long felt a nameless, profound fascination for Aztalan and Rock Lake, as though their personal destiny or past life (or both) were somehow part of this very special area in southern Wisconsin.

The Smiling Head

No less unique, although entirely different from Gordon's find, was a stone head discovered by amateur archaeologists in July 1961. They found it only half buried among a group of burial mounds in an unincorporated and little-explored area six miles northeast of the town of Muskego, about forty miles east of Aztalan. Since September 1962, it has been in the possession of the Waukesha County Historical Society. Carved from local, white dolerite, a coarse, crystalline variety of basalt, the head weighs 10.4 pounds, with an 11.3-inch diameter at the forehead, and is 11.8 inches long from crown to chin.

The object is especially unique because it depicts a smiling face. Lone, provocative parallels occur among the smiling-head figures of ancient Mexico (classic Veracruz, circa A.D. 700). Aztalan's undeniable and important links to Mesoamerica, to say nothing of the seacoast location of Veracruz, imply a southern influence at work in the Upper Midwest during the deep past. But the Wisconsin and Mexican heads are not stylistically related, and the Veracruz specimens were made of terra cotta, not stone.

The Muskego artifact is not severely weathered, prompting archaeologists to conclude that it may belong to the last Mississippian phase of Aztalan, at the earliest, or possibly as late as the early historic period of Indian occupation of Waukesha County, into the early 1800s. A high date for the stone head would be no less fascinating than assigning it to the florescence of Aztalan in the fourteenth century. The natives encountered by the first modern European settlers of southeastern Wisconsin were the Potawatomi. The German and Irish immigrants were surprised at the Caucasian faces of these "Indians." An 1859 photograph of a Potawatomi girl in traditional dress (Oklahoma Historical Society, Oklahoma City)

Smiling stone head of Muskego

shows her with dark, auburn hair and distinctly European facial features. Some researchers believe that it was this tribe, not the resident Winnebago, who were the real descendants of the civilizers of Aztalan. Their very name implies as much: "People of the Place of the Fire," suggestive of the great conflagration that utterly consumed Aztalan in A.D. 1320. The Potawatomi were, moreover, the creators of agricultural villages of large, birch-covered houses and dome-shaped wigwams, not unlike examples at the incinerated ceremonial center.

While most of the Aztalaners migrated south after abandoning their capital to the flames, perhaps a few stayed behind to reform into a new tribe. Although most investigators are reasonably sure the stone head is authentic, they complain that it was not excavated under professionally controlled conditions, and are, therefore, reluctant to wholeheartedly accept it as genuine. In any case, it seems clear that the smiling artifact belongs to the ancient Aztalaners or their immediate descendants.

The Mystery of the Cross—Solved

In my previous volume, I described an immense cross that once lay at
the foot of another lake not far from Aztalan. The earthwork in question was only one among some ten thousand effigy mounds sculptured
into the Wisconsin landscape before the fourteenth century A.D. But
this one was unique for more than its configuration. It was a perfect
cross 420 feet across and four feet thick at the arms, with a forty-four-
foot diameter at midpoint. The colossal precision of its construction at
right angles made it resemble a compass, a suggestion that hinted at its
real identity. The intellectual skill and organizational effort to create it
bespoke the surveying prowess and capable labor management of its
builders. But why did they make it?

For some reason, the cross was singularly important to the prehistoric community that sponsored its creation. Of all those other thousands of ancient earthworks that spread from the Dakotas to Georgia,
it was the most unique. But I erred in *The Lost Pyramids of Rock Lake*
when I reported that its only identical counterpart could still be found
in Ohio. David Hatcher Childress reproduced a nineteenth-century
illustration of the Tarlton Cross in *Lost Cities of North and Central America*. It was not the same as the compass-like earthwork after all.[3]

The Wisconsin effigy lay at the south end of Lake Sinissippi, about
twenty-seven airline miles north of Aztalan, to which it is in fact
directly connected by the Crawfish River. Although obliterated
around the turn of the last century, the mound was thoroughly surveyed before its destruction and we know that it was oriented to the
four cardinal directions, its designers having used the North Star as
their chief point of reference. But why such a gigantic, carefully oriented earthwork, unlike any other, was fashioned in this relatively
remote part of the state, and what it might once have signified, no
one could guess. Only its style suggested it had been fashioned by
the same effigy-mound builders who enhanced the immediate environs of Aztalan with similarly sculpted figures.

In spring 1992, I drove to Huistisford, the small town built over
the cross, to learn something about Wisconsin's vanished mystery. The
local historian could tell me nothing I did not already know. In view of
Rock Lake's sunken necropolis, I wondered if the cross did not indicate a like phenomenon in Lake Sinissippi. But a diver I met at its
shore told me that Sinissippi is more a broad section of the Crawfish
River than a real lake, averaging no more than five or six feet deep. It
has no traditions, ancient or modern, of underwater structures. Nor

has it undergone any dramatic rises or falls over the last thousand years, at least. There were no pyramids in this lake.

I stood where my best guess placed the cross and tried to imagine why the ancient ones had gone to so much trouble for the creation of this special earthwork in such an apparently insignificant location. Answer came there none. But as I drove away, the mystery still revolving in my mind, I remembered that the translation of the name, Sinissippi, from the original Algonkian is "Serpent Ore." Could the "Serpent" have represented the serpentine course of the Crawfish River and "ore" referred to the copper that was mined by the thousands of tons from the Upper Peninsula?

Consulting my road atlas, I examined Sinissippi's position relative to Isle Royale, the chief focus of the ancient copper enterprise, and Aztalan. I found no apparent correlation. But when my glance traveled down to Cahokia, the Mississippian capital that immediately preceded Aztalan, I noticed at once that Huistisford seemed to lie midway between Cahokia and Isle Royale.

Hydrological history charts, based on computerized projections of the Michigan, Wisconsin, and Illinois river systems as they appeared between A.D. 900 and 1100 (the two centuries of Cahokia's operational existence) subsequently confirmed that Lake Sinissippi lay at the precise midpoint between Isle Royale and Cahokia for anyone traveling between these two locations via the rivers which connected them. The crew and captain of an ore-laden vessel sent from Isle Royale down the Rock River toward the Mississippi River and Cahokia would have reached the exact half-way stage to their destination when they arrived at Sinissippi. Its great cross-mound marked the precise midpoint between Michigan's copper source and its metropolitan center in Illinois. This means that it was made after A.D. 900 by the prehistoric mining engineers of Cahokia, when that city's copper trade was in full swing. No other interpretation approaches a credible explanation for the Sinissippi Cross.

Physical evidence in support of Illinois miners in the Upper Peninsula was made available to me through Wayne May, the discoverer of the Aztalan trading token described above. He told me that "a multiplicity of points" positively identified as having been manufactured in Cahokia between the tenth and twelfth centuries was found at a place called Sard Point, at the heart of the old copper mining territory, on the shores of Lake Superior, between the Apostle Islands and Keweenaw. The arrowheads were too numerous for trade items and were unquestionably brought to Upper Michigan by persons from Cahokia. The significance of Sinissippi's magnificent, vanished earthwork underscores the importance too often ignored by historians of the copper commerce in prehistoric America and the extremes the ancients went to preserve it as the basis of Cahokia's economic power.

A Wisconsin Monolith

But the Sinissippi Cross was not the only mystery on dry land we tackled in 1992. The year before, Lloyd Hornbostel made a fascinating discovery on Goose Island, or Missouri Hill as it is also known, a lonely, wooded place five miles west of Rock Lake. Rarely visited, this out-of-the way spot hides an eight-foot-tall standing stone erected and roughly shaped into a manmade monolith. Its resemblance to European menhirs, particularly in Britain, is uncanny. The monolith stands atop the highest section of Missouri Hill and is surrounded by a circle of lesser stones. About a hundred feet away stands a large earth mound, perhaps ten feet tall, thirty-five feet long, and fifteen feet in diameter. It has not yet been excavated, so speculation about its identity as a burial monument remains to be confirmed. But its presence at the hilltop affirms the ancient significance of the whole site.

During my first visit to Missouri Hill, I found some evidence that helped establish the precinct's prehistoric credibility beyond question. A few feet from the tall monolith, I noticed what appeared to be faint drawings on the face of a nearby boulder. On closer examination, they proved to be two petroglyphs, much weathered but still plainly discernible. One depicts a serpent wrapped around an oval. The other is more abstract, although somewhat resembling the so-called "weeping eye" motif found on artifacts from Oklahoma to the Gateway of the Sun at Lake Titicaca, in Peru. My first impression of the more recognizable of the two was that it represented the serpent-and-egg theme belonging to a worldwide, deeply prehistoric mystery healing cult, whose symbolism was encountered from ancient Greece, as the emblem of Asclepius, the mythic father of medicine, to the Great Serpent Mound, a 1,200-foot-long effigy atop another hill, this one in the Ohio Valley.

But if the petroglyph does illustrate the serpent-and-egg theme, then its implications for nearby Rock Lake could be decisive. The image of a snake disgorging an egg represents the oldest known cosmology. It signified the demiurge, the primal act of creation, the Cosmic Egg, a metaphor for the origin of life, while the snake was the

Ancient megalith atop Missouri Hill, eight miles west of Rock Lake

eternal power that brought it forth. Its most famous form today is the caduceus, the magical scepter of the god Mercury, recognized world-wide as the emblem of medical practice. It was also the symbol of the Pelasgians, those pre-Greek Sea Peoples identified as Bronze Age voyagers from Atlantis. Hesiod, the early mythographer of Greek prehistory, wrote that "the Pelasgians claimed their birth from the fangs of Ophion, the great primeval serpent."[4]

An Atlantean connection linking the copper-rich Upper Peninsula to Rock Lake and the mid-ocean city is strongly implied by abundant, suggestive data. Perhaps the small, faded petroglyph atop Missouri Hill was left by copper miners from Atlantis when they passed its great monolith. Interestingly, its accompanying petroglyph, the weeping eye, is associated with the word for "deluge," even in some of the Aymara dialects of the Andes. Perhaps it signifies the catastrophe that either destroyed Atlantis or inundated the necropolis under Rock Lake.

Cave Painting

In my previous volume, I portrayed Aztalan as the capital of a political power that stretched across Wisconsin and into northern Illinois, a conclusion derided by most mainstream scholars, who regard the enclosure as an entity of and by itself, without any real influence beyond its immediate environs. Since publication, I learned of two other Aztalan-like sites, one in Joe Davis County, near Potosi, Wisconsin, known as the Frank Edwards site, a hundred airline miles west of Rock Lake, and the Lindy Site, in northern Illinois, a further twenty-five miles south. According to Dr. Robert Salzer, Professor of Anthropology at Beloit College, the two are Late Mississippian outposts of Aztalan. While smaller and without temple mounds, they featured stockaded, lime-plastered walls identical to those which made up the larger enclosure. Moreover, they were built shortly after Aztalan began its final major phase, in A.D. 1100.

Dr. Salzer has also undertaken remarkable research at a cave near Muscoda, where vibrant rock paintings of the ancient Aztalaners were found about ten years ago. Muscoda lies some eighty airline miles from Aztalan. These three important sites clearly demonstrate that, far from having been some provincial town isolated in the southern part of the state, Aztalan was the cultural and administrative centerpiece of a political power that dominated part of the upper Midwest for two hundred years.

*Frank Joseph at the remains of a circular stone mound at Missouri Hill,
a few miles from Rock Lake, which has its own identical structures*

But the Gottschall Site at Muscoda suggests the Aztalaners spread
their commercial and cultural ties beyond Illinois, as far away as Oklahoma. There, at a pyramidal complex known as Spiro Mounds, on
the Arkansas River, shells were artistically engraved depicting the
same figures and even in the same style as those discovered in the
Wisconsin cave.

As James P. Valiga writes (1987), "Comparing the figures of the
Gottschall rock paintings with the Spiro style shell engravings, one is
struck by the close similarities in the styles used." He then lists eight
points of comparison between the Wisconsin and Oklahoma artworks.
"These eight similarities present a high degree of correlation between
the artistic styles used at the two sites."[5] Apparently, Aztalan was not
some lone outpost of the Late Mississippian tradition, but part of, if
not indeed the capital of, a vast civilization that dominated the Midwest as far south as Oklahoma. The Spiro Mound people were known
to operate thirty-foot boats carrying three masts of sail made from
woven mats, so they certainly possessed the maritime technology necessary to visit faraway Aztalan on a regular basis.

The Head of Red Horn

A most remarkable find was made on July 20, 1992, when a field archaeologist for the Canadian government involved in ongoing research at the Gottschall rock shelter, discovered an anciently carved human head, the only one of its kind ever found in the state. The twenty-six-centimeter sandstone sculpture has been tentatively dated to a thousand years ago, just when Aztalan began to flourish eighty miles away. For the first time, we look upon the face of one of the mysterious civilizers of eleventh-century Wisconsin.

The same rock shelter has been directly linked to Aztalan through the native American legend of Red Horn, which was portrayed in more than forty cave paintings discovered in 1974 and since researched by Dr. Salzer. His supposition was confirmed when he uncovered pottery shards in the cave; they unquestionably belonged to vessels manufactured in Aztalan.

Miraculously, traces of paint still appeared on the fragile sandstone sculpture. The unworked back of the artwork implied it was meant to have originally worn some kind of headgear or helmet, while notches at the base of the neck were made to fit the head into the trunk of a complete statue or perhaps a stylized pole. The find, for all its thousand years of age, strangely suggests a foreign presence in prehistoric Wisconsin. Pre-sixteenth-century Indians rarely if ever worked in stone portraiture, certainly never on the level of sophistication evident in the Gottschall find. Moreover, its facial features do not reflect an aboriginal countenance.

Perhaps the sandstone sculpture was meant to portray the hero, Red Horn, whose image appears on the cave wall. The rock paintings depict an episode from his legend, which mythically parallels our description of an Atlanto-European arrival in ancient Wisconsin and probably connects the Gottschall site to prehistoric events at Rock Lake.

Myth as History

The episode in question concerns the hero's conflict with the giants. Tradition portrayed them as men and women of particularly tall stature and superior physical strength, who lived behind the high walls of "a great lodge" where they engaged in many sporting events. Dr. Salzer believes these giants of Wisconsin oral history were none other than the inhabitants of Aztalan. Indeed, their high-walled ceremonial center enclosed a large plaza, were games of all kinds were played. The giants were described in the legend as red haired, a provocative feature, which, together with their tall stature, suggests European origins. A European provenance is, in fact, emphasized when the last giant survivors go back "across the seas."[6] Appropriately, the few adult burials excavated in Aztalan revealed persons of exceptional height.

Red Horn is eventually defeated by the giants and decapitated. Later, his son retrieves his skull and uses it to restore his father to life. Ritual beheading was among the magical themes running throughout Aztalan, from the headless giant unearthed there to a nearby colossal earthwork depicting a decapitated figure. The Red Horn story not only connects Muscoda to Aztalan, but suggests that a skull cult practiced at both sites evoked some ritual concept of regeneration and rebirth. As his cycle continues, it begins to describe the fate of Aztalan. In it, the giants were mostly killed in retributive wars and their corpses piled up behind the walls of their city. "It made a big blaze, for the giants were very fat."[7] Aztalan was, historically, destroyed by an all-consuming fire.

Interestingly, Red Horn himself was portrayed as a mixed descendant of the light-haired giants. His name was drawn from his own crop of red hair. And there is a curious passage in his legend, when he spits on his hand, then moves it over his brother's hair, which turns suddenly blond.[8] The incident suggests that they were both descended from a racially alien people, whose red and yellow hair could only have belonged to prehistoric travelers from Europe. As Dr. Scherz wrote, the Red Horn story "documents a real historic event, embellished for dramatic effect."[9]

The Gottschall cave in which the narrative rock paintings of Red Horn appear was undoubtedly chosen by the shamans of long ago as a place to generate spiritual power through mythic drama perceived in the natural environment: "Researchers accidentally discovered that music played within the shelter in the area of the paintings could be heard at the top of the bluff near the open field, but a generator running near the rock shelter could not. Sounds from the valley were also heard in the shelter near the paintings, yet could not be heard outside the rock shelter. This acoustical effect may prove to be an indicator that this shelter could have been selected for ceremonial use at one time."[10]

Doubtless, the Gottschall shelter was a sacred site, at which both visual and auditory stimuli, in the cave's unusual acoustic properties and the colorful dramatization of myth among its rock art, combined with the religious theater of music, dance, declamation, and other ritual behavior, augmented by consciousness-altering narcotics to produce powerful personal experiences. The wall paintings could not have been created before 2000 B.C., because the smooth rock face on which they appear did not exist until a major earthquake "caused the bottom of the roof to fracture and collapse."[11] Coincidentally, scuba divers in 1989 located an earthquake fault on the bottom of Rock Lake, at the north end. One wonders if the lake and the cave were linked by some tremendous seismic event that left scars at both sites.

Dive to a Sunken Pyramid

The shock of cold water rushing into my wet suit, as I plunged down through Rock Lake on May 14, 1994, was not so traumatic as I had anticipated. More importantly, subsurface visibility for this usually turbid body of water was extraordinarily good. I could see clearly in every direction for almost thirty feet through the emerald hues of subsurface twilight.

Since 1987, my colleagues and I had scoured the bottom of this lovely lake in search of its legendary "lost pyramids," remembered in local Winnebago tradition as the sunken "rock tepees" of an alien tribe. After years of persistent, largely fruitless dives, our high-tech sonar instruments did indeed verify a number of sometimes gargantuan manmade stone structures lying below the surface, often at relatively shallow depths, sometimes much further down. But always we discovered them along former streambeds or ancient beach levels, just where one would expect to find such monuments. From all the evidence we collected and shared with scholars from Wisconsin and Illinois universities, the picture of a sunken civilization in the Midwest began to emerge.

But obtaining good photographs of the underwater monuments was always extremely problematical, owing to Rock Lake's usually poor subsurface visibility. As I descended to the target area identified by our sonar, I hoped that the lake would cooperate, at least this once. Three fathoms above me in our small boat was Lloyd Hornbostel, who has the best "feeling" for Rock Lake of anyone I know. Operating as much by instinct as with sonar, he directed us to an area virtually ignored in all our previous expeditions, in a west-central section of the lake.

Almost at once, our instrument registered a small hill rising steeply from the bottom. It was accompanied by a very curious feature

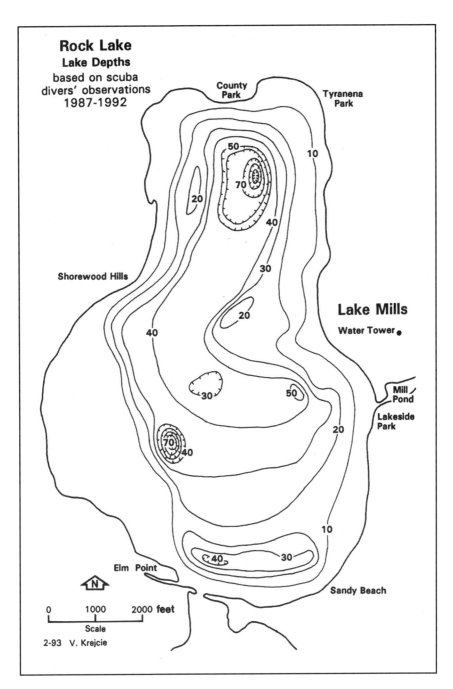

Rock Lake lake depths

map courtesy of Valerie W. Krejcie

Key to Map on Opposite Page

1. The Temple of the Moon, or Limnatis Pyramid
2. The Kennedy Structure
3. Small stone platform mound
4. Zeke's Wall fronted by pyramidal structure
5. Line of single stones
6. Chimney-like conical structures at the edge of the ancient shoreline
7. Headless Man and Turtle effigy mounds
8. Bass Rock Bar-I
9. Larger volcano-like stone mound
10. Annular stone mound
11. Ridge-top stone mound
12. Collapsed circular structure of stone from which man-made brick was retrieved
13. Smaller volcano-like stone mound
14. Delta-shaped mound, the largest known feature in Rock Lake
15. Max Nohl's Cone, largest of the known conical pyramids
16. Wreck of a small boat

southeast of the sonar target was a circular, narrow hole that went straight down through the thirty-foot bottom of the lake to seventy-two feet. Having found this peculiar site by accident seven years previously, I had never been able to relocate it. Most researchers, aware that no natural forces could be responsible for such a perfectly vertical depression, believe it is an ancient well.

Their supposition was powerfully underscored the moment I reached the east side of the hill, about five meters down. There I saw what appeared to be the foundation of a circular building. Less than ten feet in diameter, it was composed of boulders arranged into a ring formation. But as I readied my camera, my flipper accidentally stirred

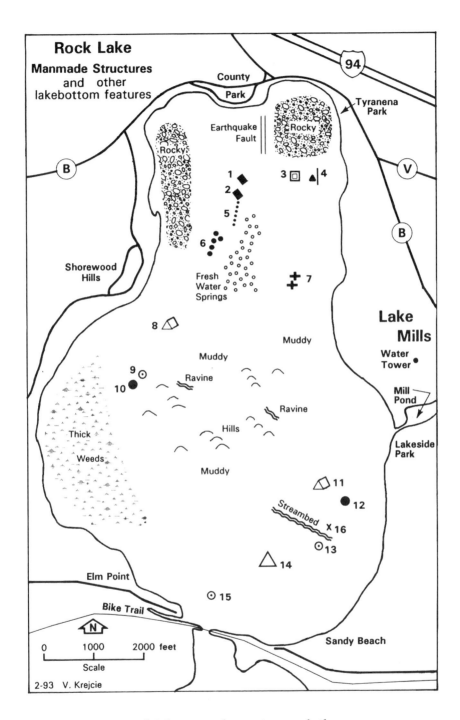

*Rock Lake manmade structures and other
lake bottom features*

map courtesy of Valerie W. Krejcie

up a cloud of mud—into which the stone structure vanished! I decided to allow the silt time to resettle, so I slowly swam around the south end of the hill, looking for other structures. Visibility was about the best I could hope for in Rock Lake, allowing me long, clear vistas of this weird world below.

The small but steep hill was itself an anomaly. It looked like little more than a high collection of stones, many thousands of them, surrounded in all directions as far as I could see by the vast panorama of a dark brown mud bottom, its shadowy parameters defined by spooky darkness.

But I was not alone. A large bass, at least three feet long, volunteered as my diving buddy. Swimming a slow, parallel course, just beyond arm's reach, he eyed me with skeptical curiosity, as though to ask, "What kind of a clumsy fish are you?"

Having found nothing anomalous by the time we reached the west side of the hill, I decided to cut back across its summit toward the east; I was anxious to photograph that stone circle and imagined the silt must have had sufficient time to settle down. But as my fishy companion and I rose over the crest of the hill, I was startled to see a pyramidal structure gradually materialize at the very top. Even from about thirty feet away, its configuration was entirely distinct in the silent, turquoise environment. As I hurried closer, the monument grew even more impressive in its details. The stones around its base were quite large; I guessed they weighed some two hundred pounds each. Some of them appeared to be cut into cube shapes, but there was no trace of mortar. Although in a ruinous condition, the pyramid was nicely made; not some crude heap of stones, but fitted together with thought and purpose.

The Sunken Island

I was so startled by my first sight of this lovely apparition, my rational mind refused to admit the obvious: that it was manmade. It was no diver's hoax (the obvious weight of its base stones and the time and energy required to make such a thing ruled out fraud), but had been constructed by someone a very long time ago, when Rock Lake was much shallower. I checked my depth gauge: twenty feet. Remarkable! That was the precise depth at which most of the stone structures had been found elsewhere in the lake.

Apparently, this underwater hill was centuries ago a little island, its summit dry land. It was probably revered by the ancient inhabitants of the Rock Lake area as sacred ground. Islands are almost uni-

Underwater pyramid at Rock Lake

versally regarded by nature-oriented peoples as holy territories, because they are separated from the land by a watery barrier, usually representing death or the next world. Perhaps this pyramid was built by them for sacred purposes. Over the course of time, or due to causes not yet understood, the lake levels rose, drowning the structure.

It did indeed stand at the very top of the hill, from which I could look down in all directions. I got as close to it as I dared, because its arrangement of stones seemed delicate, even fragile. Hovering carefully about three feet overhead, I looked down into what appeared to be a dark chamber at the very core of the pyramid. But part of the structure had collapsed, perhaps only giving the illusion of some internal feature. Further investigation should be able to make a determination. In any case, the structure stands about five feet tall, with a lower diameter of perhaps seven feet; the absolute bottom of the structure was hidden in mud, to what depth I had no way to guess.

Although certainly pyramidal, in overall configuration it is essentially a squat cone, circular at the base, somewhat resembling the shape of a Hershey's chocolate "kiss." However, the structure's original appearance may have been substantially different from the impression made by its presently dilapidated status. The stones with which it was made were almost certainly taken from the hill it dominates, since similarly large examples are strewn in great profusion in close proximity, although the hill itself is located in a virtual desert of stone-free mud.

As I excitedly set up the camera, my bass companion obligingly slid into view, posing motionless before the sunken pyramid. Apologizing for my dwindling air supply, I began my ascent, unable to keep my eyes off the wonderful and mysterious structure falling away below me. Back at the surface, I yelled the good news to Lloyd. His wide-ranging expertise did more than make our marvelous find possible: after taking precise bearings on the site, he learned that my camera had sprung a leak and the film was in serious danger of damage. Lloyd rushed over to a photographer friend and, together, drying each frame by hand, they saved our precious evidence.

The little subsurface hill we found was undoubtedly an island occupied by someone when Rock Lake was at least twenty feet lower than present. Its apparent "well," the circular foundation on its east side, and the stone monument at its summit all bespeak human impact. Since the area is not regarded as good for fishing, Lloyd speculates that the structure's ruinous condition is probably less the result of fisherman's anchors than ice, which worked its way back and forth over the pyramid during the course of at least several winters as lake levels rose.

In any case, our find poses more questions than it answers: Who could have made such a thing, how long ago, and why? What lay (or still may lie) inside its lightless "chamber"? Until further visits to the stone enigma sitting alone atop its underwater hill, the lost pyramid of Rock Lake keeps its age-old peace.

Underwater Explosions

Scuba divers have also experienced strange phenomena in Rock Lake that they have encountered nowhere else. Several times in the course of some one hundred dives there, I distinctly heard the sounds of explosions while down around forty feet or more. In September 1994, I not only heard the explosions but saw them: mushroom-like clouds of silt suddenly erupted from the lake bottom. After a lecture I gave at the Fort Atkinson Library that summer, a man in the audience told me that he too, had heard the mysterious booming. So the "explosions" were not all that uncommon, however inexplicable.

After sharing my experiences with Lloyd, he offered this explanation in personal correspondence:

> Divers working in Rock Lake have seen what appears to be some sort of underwater burst with much rising silt and a column not unlike a miniature mushroom cloud. A muffled explosion noise is also associated with the phenomenon. This condition is caused by the release of methane gas generated under anaerobic (without oxygen) conditions by the decomposition of organic matter. Methane bacteria—methenagens—reduce organic matter and produce the methane gas as a by-product of decomposition. The gas collects under a blanket of lake bottom silt, and, when the gas bubble is of a sufficient size to lift the silt layer, the burst results. The same process operates in swamps; when the surface gas is ignited by thunderstorms (lightning strikes), the spectacular fireballs called Saint Elmo's Fire occur. Saint Elmo was the heavenly patron of sailors, and a ship sailing in warm, shallow seas during thunderstorm activity often initiated the fire with a lightning strike to the mast. Sailors were terrified to see fireballs rolling about the ship's deck. Essentially, the same process is going on under the lake.

Despite Lloyd's scientific explanation, the underwater explosions at Rock Lake add another dimension of mystery for divers below that unusual body of water.

Our investigations have unraveled much of the mystery that belongs to Rock Lake, but many more enigmas still await explanation.

Restored wall at Aztalan with Pyramid of the Sun in background

·8·

Outposts of Aztalan

*There is no permanence. Do we build a house to stand for-
ever? It is only the nymph of the dragon-fly who sheds her
larva and sees the sun in his glory. From the days of old, there
is no permanence.*

—*From the Sumerian* Epic of Gilgamesh,
second millennium B.C.

The Aztalaners' sphere of influence—politically and culturally—was not limited to their twenty-one-square-acre ceremonial center on the banks of the Crawfish River. In previous
chapters, we learned that they were also responsible for the Muscoda
Cave in western Wisconsin and the Man Mound outside Baraboo.
While the precise limits of their power cannot be defined, we do
know that they imported goods from as far away as the Gulf of Mexico, the West Indies, Georgia's Atlantic coast, and the Ohio Valley. We
may, however, begin to gather an impression of the extent of the
polity, the governing state they created, by investigating three
related sites that appear to have marked the prehistoric kingdom's
immediate boundaries.

To the north, the Aztalaners extended their reach to the rich copper mines of the Upper Great Lakes, their economic reason for being.
Year-round settlement was prevented by the hard-snow line, which
occurs about a hundred miles north of the ceremonial enclosure.

The Aztalaners were known to have imported milkstone from Illinois for use as hoes, and it is here that their southernmost outpost may still be found.

Less than a two-hour drive from Chicago, a lonely boulder stands atop its hill overlooking thousands of commuters speeding on the expressway below from their suburban homes to jobs in the city and back again each work day. Absorbed in the mundane affairs of modern survival, they are oblivious to the magical monolith that still points its unchanging finger at the sky, just as it did for many centuries before the suburbanites' forefathers came to northern Illinois. This part of the state comprises flat farmland, so the appearance of even the fifty-foot hill crowned with its solitary stone seems outstanding.

Across the road is an adjacent hill of almost equal height. In fact, the site is referred to as "Indian Hills." The stone in question stands at the highest point around for as far as the eye can see. Despite the "Indian" association, Sauk tribes which inhabited the area until the early nineteenth century did not haul the one-ton burden up to its lofty position. They did, however, venerate it as a manitou, or sacred object, left behind by "shamans of the moon," who set up the hill-top altar in thanks for their survival from the Great Flood. The ancient shamans suffused the precinct with part of their spirit before moving on to the north.

The stone is probably a local glacial remnant from the last Ice Age, but worked by human beings to shape its pointy top— although a hundred centuries of continuous weathering have effaced all traces of human modification, if any. In any case, getting the massive monolith moved up the steeply inclined slope to the top must have been a collective endeavor of no small effort. In fact, given the known technological limitations of pre-Columbian man, we can only speculate how its removal to the hilltop was achieved. It is the same dilemma we face when confronted by the creation of Britain's Stonehenge.

Nor does our comparison with the more famous site on the Salisbury Plain end there. In the Arthurian tradition of Stonehenge, Merlin supposedly levitated the heavy monoliths through the air and set them up in concentric circles. A surviving legend among the Sauk recounts that the ancient shamans, through the power of their magic, floated the Indian Hills Stone from its home at the bottom of a river and set it gently down to face and pay homage to the moon goddess. And as the lunar alignments of Stonehenge are generally acknowledged today, so the Illinois monolith is oriented to the most northerly rising of the moon.

Indian Hill crowned with its moon-oriented stone

The phenomenon is still observable from the adjacent hill across the expressway. Judging from its precise position and the substantial physical labor that went into erecting it, the Indian Hills Stone apparently meant a great deal to whoever set it up.

While any connection between a Midwestern monolith and Stonehenge may seem far-fetched, Sauk traditions of moon-worshipping shamans and ancient European myths of a prehistoric worldwide civilization should at least give us pause for reflection.

The Magic Moon

Once each year, the moon seems to rise from out of the Indian Hills Stone itself and then balance momentarily at its apex before resuming its voyage across the night sky. At such magical moments, the stone does indeed resemble an "altar of the moon," as the Sauk tradition recounted. The orientation must have been particularly important to prehistoric Americans. Some seventy miles north of the Indian Hills Stone, in southern Wisconsin, lies Aztalan's Pyramid of the Moon; this earthen temple mound is likewise oriented to the most northerly rising of the moon. The same alignment occurs much farther away, in east-central Ohio, at the gargantuan Newark mound group, which

The Indian Hills Stone

Spirit stone of Devil's Lake

was designed and used as an enormous ritualized center by an unknown people, about two thousand years ago.

The observation of the moon at its most northerly point undoubtedly heralded an annual universal beginning of some kind associated with the resurgence of female energy. But lunar worship was not confined to female disciples. Rather, the Eternal Feminine, as Goethe portrayed at the end of *Faust,* is part of the sacred duality that pervades all things: aggressive-receptive, extrovert-introvert, conscious-subconscious, etc. Moon energy is especially associated with psychic phenomena—dreams, telepathy, healing, clairvoyance, clairaudience—all the elements that belong to the shamanistic experience recalled by the native Sauk.

The ancients certainly used the Indian Hills Stone for the practice of their spiritual craft. Interestingly, when the moon rises at its northernmost point on the horizon, it exerts its strongest gravitational pull on our planet. Astronomers refer to this attraction as the maximum lunar declination. Seismologists regard the moon's optimum effect as a cause of earthquakes, which are sometimes provoked when the lunar declination pulls on unstable plates beneath the planet's surface. Criminologists know that peak periods of violent human behavior coincide with the full moon.

Of course, the ancient observers who set up the Indian Hills Stone may have been interested in the most northerly lunar rise simply because the moon appears largest at that time. Whether or not they knew somehow about maximum lunar declination, the prehistoric shamans at least seem to have understood that the moon extended its greatest power at its northernmost positions, a power that influenced human affairs, particularly those relating to psychic experience.

Phenomena at Devil's Lake
Aztalan's western influence has already been described at the Muscoda Cave and Baraboo's Man Mound. Not far from this anthropomorphic effigy mound is an extraordinarily beautiful lake that was likewise part of the state's prehistoric drama.

This Wisconsin body of water was done a lingering injustice when early settlers renamed it "Devil's Lake." Known to countless generations of native Americans as "Spirit Lake," its shimmering beauty is diametrically opposed to everything Satanic. But early American zealots, convinced that they alone were true believers, demoted the deity of the resident Indians to archfiend. Despite its misnomer and its status as the greatest tourist draw in the state, Spirit Lake is a major sacred center in which human energies and Nature's own genius loci combine to make wonderful magic.

Actually, for all the tens of thousands of tourists who descend on the lake each year, the whole area is much improved over past conditions. It is a well-regulated park, a welcome change after the crass materialism that littered its shores earlier in the century. Today, the lake and its environs are clean, safe, and unobstructed by commercialism. Even so, those seeking the unique spiritual ambience of the lake are advised to avoid the lake during the tourist season. April and May in the spring and mid-Indian summer in the fall are the optimum times for visitors hoping to encounter the inherent qualities of the sacred site. Certainly, the most ideal moments occur at the vernal and autumnal equinoxes.

Spirit Lake radiates beauty of a very unusual kind. Although only three miles across, it is almost completely surrounded by high cliffs of purple quartzite, honeycombed with caves and adorned with

Devil's Lake, Wisconsin

the abstractly fashioned sculpture of eons. High trails wind through pine woods encircling the water and wander off into additional hundreds of acres of untouched forest. Some of the views, particularly toward the north, are so spectacular, they are more characteristic of Colorado than Wisconsin. Dusk suffuses the site with a singular enchantment, as the purple quartzite cliffs glow in the direct rays of the setting sun. Although the lake appears to have been created by a colossal meteorite impact, volcanic forces, or some such violent geologic action, scholars believe it is the remnant of a vast sea that covered the entire state seven million years ago.

The naturally numinous aura of Spirit Lake was not lost on the original inhabitants. They created magnificent earth sculptures above its shoreline. At the western end may still be seen the prehistoric effigy mounds of bears. On the opposite shore, the graceful geoglyph of a gull angles its eighty-foot wingspread parallel to the water. At the center of the bird's head, like a third eye, lies a remarkable stone, a large, somewhat cubic quartz. Its dark purple alternates in a close pattern of lighter vein, generating a vibratory effect, as though the specimen were rippling with fabulous earth energies. In the middle of the bird mound lie the half-buried ruins of an ancient cairn, a small, circular monument. A tree has grown up through its center, and roots entwine some of the stones.

The waters of Spirit Lake are clear and cold, being spring-fed. A nearby scuba shop rents a variety of equipment for divers, who are urged to bring their wet suits.

Spirit Lake doubtless possessed its haunting, numinous quality when its prehistoric inhabitants first sculpted their earth-effigy mounds along its shores between the first and fifth centuries A.D. But why did they choose to fashion the images of bears at one end and a bird at the other? The selection of these particular animals and their positions represents a high spiritual significance that may be discerned from observation of the mounds themselves and their interdependent relationship with the natural environment. The effigies may be seen year round, but they have their special days when they exhibit magical qualities not visible at any other time.

Bird and Bear Mounds

A case in point is the gull mound. While the shape can be made out from ground level, the figure may be appreciated in its entirety only from a high vantage point. Fortunately, such a perspective still exists for the modern visitor. It is a ledge jutting out from the cliff face toward the mound two hundred feet below. The ledge may be easily reached by following the trail. The broad outcropping was a sacred precinct for the ancient inhabitants and their tribal leaders.

From this natural precipice, the gull effigy should theoretically appear in all its sculpted symmetry. But it is invisible, save only once each year, at dusk on the day of the vernal equinox. As the sun goes down on the first day of spring, and for a few days thereafter, the giant bird far below materializes and seems to be streaking toward the lake. The dramatic spectacle is created when the direct rays of the sun at twilight delineate the terraglyph with shadows, lengthening and spreading as evening approaches. The creators of this earthwork deliberately and precisely oriented it to achieve this wonderful vision, which, like the special effect of some cosmic mechanism, has been faithfully reproducing itself over the last two thousand years. At ground level, the shadows seem meaningless, but from the cliff, they make the effigy live.

A like drama occurs at the opposite end of the lake, when the bear mounds are similarly delineated by the sun rising on the shortest day of the year. They complete the meaning of the mysticism instituted at Spirit Lake so many centuries ago. Their alignment with the solstice signified the opening of winter, the season during which bears hibernate. So, too, the coastal bird mound oriented to sundown of the vernal equinox marks the beginning of spring, when the birds do indeed return to Spirit Lake.

Certainly, the ancient residents did not go to such lengths in the creation of these alignment mounds for frivolous purposes. Even a purely economic intention for the effigies as agricultural calendars seems unlikely. Rather, they were sculpted as outsized theatrical devices to inspire a whole community's sense of awe in the cosmic cycle and to make them feel part of that eternal drama.

The Muscoda Cave, Man Mound, and nearby Devil's Lake define the westward limits of Aztalan's power. Illinois' Indian Hills Stone stands as the discernible extent of the Aztalaners' southern influence. These are the remnants of a lost civilization, the outposts of a vanished people, who dominated an important region of America's Midwest 180 years before Columbus set sail from Spain.

.9.

The Scuba Inventor
and the Indian Teacher

Facts do not cease to exist because they are ignored.
                                                    —Aldous Huxley

The thousands of divers in the U.S. and abroad who today enjoy the world below the surface cannot guess that the inventor of their scuba gear tested the first of its kind in Wisconsin's Rock Lake, as part of his search for the sunken pyramids, more than fifty years ago. His name was Max Gene Nohl, and his revolutionary contribution to underwater exploration was announced in a feature article by Victor S. Taylor. Himself an intrepid investigator of the subsurface mystery, Taylor's story appears in *The Lost Pyramids of Rock Lake*. His report is reprinted here with the kind permission of the *Lake Mills Leader*, where it ran for the first time in the October 12, 1937, edition, under the heading, "Diver Thrilled by Finding First Rock Lake 'Pyramid'; Further Trips to be Made."

> The quest for a forgotten city, a forgotten race, or revelation of new examples of the prehistoric Aztalan civilization will follow in the wake of further investigation of the mysterious stone cone, more familiarly known by its misnomer—"pyramid"—on the bottom of Rock Lake by Max Gene Nohl, Milwaukee diver, whose ultimate quest is the torpedoed *Lusitania*, off the Irish coast. Nohl

has described in full his discovery of the mysterious cone on the bottom of Jefferson County's second largest lake."

First Underwater Find

"We found the cone Sunday, October 10th, as a climax to two months of searching," said the Milwaukeean. "Our first attempts at location were from the air. Waiting for favorable weather conditions, we flew out from Milwaukee numerous times and also accompanied Dr. F.S. Morgan in one of his flights, but we had little success in seeing far enough down into the water, because of the dirty conditions of the water caused by high winds. We also tried a hydroscope, arranged to permit vision while the boat is under way, but we had no luck with this."

Nohl, whose discovery of 36 images near the great pyramids south of Mexico City spurred his interest in the local quest, said that dragging became the obvious indicated means. "Our first drag was a bottom drag, but this proved highly impractical, because of the dense weed growth on the floor of the lake. Man, I never saw so many weeds," said Nohl. "We fouled our drag immediately and had to change tactics, so we tried a drag consisting of a line bellowing out from two weights towed behind two boats, about 150 feet apart, these weights being set about 12 feet beneath the surface. This worked all right until we stopped moving, then the drag sank to the bottom and fouled."

Nohl laughed ruefully at the memories of many futile tries to locate the cone. "Well, our final drag consisted of a light low-resistance wire held about 14 feet beneath the surface between our two boats about 200 feet apart. This wire was held down by a metal frame and ran through an eye at one boat so that it could be tended to take up or let out slack as the boats moved together or apart. With this device we found the 'pyramid.'"

Nohl also described the attempts made to locate the cone by diving. "Diving for the cone, we tried for the first time the new self-contained open diving helmet just completed by Ive Vestrem, my associate, and myself. This is the first self-contained open diving helmet in existence and utilizes the same principles as the self-contained deep-water diving suit. In either of these, the diver can go down without any connections to the surface—no pump or hose—and also have the tremendous advantages of our recently discovered helium-oxygen atmospheres," said Nohl.

"When I found the structure, however, I swam down in the 'lung'. This lung weighs 14 pounds, is completely self-contained and uses a helium-oxygen mixture which will permit diving to the depth of 250 feet or will sustain life in any unbreathable medium up to a pressure of 110 pounds per square inch. Now, this lung is designed so that a man is inert in the water—no weight or no buoyancy—and permits him to swim around like a fish. To my knowledge, it is the only thing of its kind in the world," said the explorer.

Description of the Pyramid

"The lung really helped me find the pyramid. Swimming with the lung, I didn't have to touch the bottom to stir up ooze, as would have been inevitable with the diving suit. Boy, what a thrill when I found that cone, the real thrill of a life-time," said Nohl. "The thing rises up from a 36-foot bottom to within seven feet of the surface. A deposit of ooze has collected at the base and penetration of this with my hand proved that the structure continued on down below the lake bottom. The actual shape? Well, it's a truncated cone," said Nohl. "And its approximate dimensions are three feet diameter at the top; bottom diameter, 18 feet; altitude, 29 feet. The construction is of smooth stones set in a mortar. Yes, absolutely, I'm convinced it's manmade. A thin, greenish scum covers a part of the cone. How did it get there? Either when the lake was inordinately low, or when the lake was still a part of that old river bed from Lake Winnebago to Lake Koshkonong."

Nohl isn't hesitant about advancing his ideas as to what people built the structure. "Look at the structures at Aztalan—the eight cones covered by the present mounds. All I know is that their structural design is identical with that cone we found on the bottom of Rock Lake. I think that tells the story." And what the story will further reveal must wait until Rock Lake dons its winter garb of ice, for when that happens, Nohl and Vestrem will bring their complete deep-sea diving apparatus and descend through a hole in the ice to make a thorough and leisurely inspection of territory adjacent to the mound in search of similar structures. The delay in further search is occasioned by the lack of a big enough boat here to launch their 250 pounds of diving suit from. The divers will take many pictures during their winter quest.

"Please tell the skeptics that I'll give them every opportunity to go down with us and see for themselves," concluded Nohl. "After all, the old truth holds—seeing is believing. And let me credit Claude Wilson, the man who made the original report of the cone, with nearly exact directions as to its location."

The Search Goes On

In the months and years which followed the publication of Victor Taylor's article, the planned ice dive did indeed take place, but with only partial success. The conical pyramid was promptly re-located, but underwater visibility was too poor for additional exploration, although the first photographs of the structure were taken by Nohl. Due to insufficient light and turbid conditions beneath the ice, he was not able to stand back far enough from the subject for the view finder to capture it in its entirety. Consequently, he had to approach the cone so closely, it appeared in his photographs as nothing more than an indistinct stone wall, or rather part of a wall.

World War II soon put an end to all further investigations of Rock Lake, but Nohl continued to improve his underwater "lung" and would have undoubtedly gone on to wonderful personal success with it had he and his wife not met their untimely deaths together in an automobile crash after the war. But the product of his genius was taken up by others, until today it is the means by which scuba divers visit the sunken monuments he first discovered so many years ago.

Claude Wilson, mentioned at the close of the article, was the first person to see the subsurface structure with his brother, Lee, from the side of their rowboat. In 1900, while they drifted over Rock Lake during a drought that lowered water levels and greatly improved visibility, the pair sighted the object. Claude eventually became the mayor of Lake Mills. The cone Nohl found was rediscovered by sonar in the winter of 1989, at the far south end of the lake, on a line between the old railroad trestle and the water tower. Barely visible in Nohl's day, it has since become impossible to see, because the trench in which it stands has entirely silted up over the last several decades, completely burying the structure. The sonar signal was able to penetrate the accumulated silt, however, and repeated passes over the target affirmed its identity. Its rediscoverers promptly christened it "Max Nohl's Cone."

The summer before his conical structure appeared on our sonar, an electronic sweep of the bottom of Rock Lake revealed an enormous monument its finders first referred to as the Limnatis Pyramid. Limnatis was the Roman moon goddess, Diana, in her role as the protectress of sacred lakes. We chose this appropriate deity to signify our reverence for the ancient ones who built the great sepulcher and who very likely still lie in its watery tomb. But we did not consciously realize at the time that the reference we used to describe the sunken structure was virtually the same title bestowed upon it in the deep

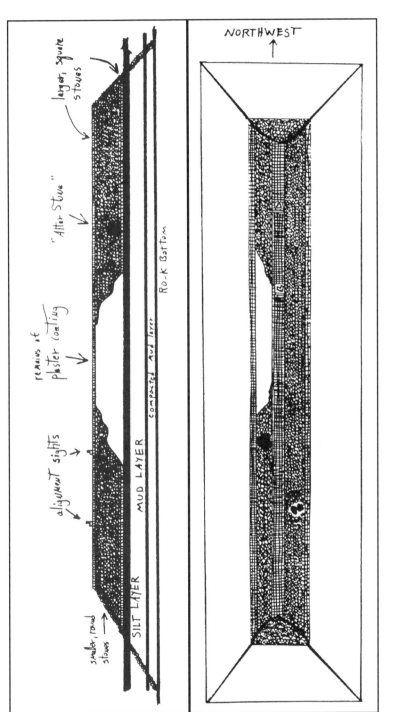

Limnatis Pyramid
Top: Lateral view; Bottom: Top view

past. It was made known two years after our discovery. Since then, our "coincidental" christening of the monument has been interpreted by psychics involved in ongoing research at Rock Lake to mean that we were subconsciously "picking up" on the spiritual energies, vibrations or echoes of the place during the course of our investigations.

In any case, such a close similarity between our modern reference and the ancient name is remarkable and worth pursuing. That this monument and its original name still live today in the oral traditions of native Americans, after perhaps 3,500 years, is wonderful proof that the stone mound observed by divers is indeed a manmade site.

The Voice of the Elder
This valuable evidence was made available by Professor James Scherz, whose own contributions to historical enlightenment are as many as they are priceless. Dr. Scherz is professor of surveying at the University of Wisconson (Madison). The following account was written in his own words and is published here for the first time:

> If we place prime focus on the mysterious rock structures of Rock Lake we cannot do so honestly without relating to the Indian stories and the possibility that they go back thousands of years.
>
> It was late at night, my eyes were drooping, but my Indian teacher continued to talk and tell of the times when the Chinetec (Chinese people) and the Redbeards came, and the diseases that followed, and how some of the priests came to Wisconsin fleeing disease from Mexico, with artifacts containing gold that he showed me. These were found in the secret traditions of many Midwest tribes, not only his. He said the area in Wisconsin was always important to many people. They came to the "Temple of the Moon," or the "Lake of the Moon," or the "Place of the Moon." He said that is the place in Rock Lake that is now flooded. Rock structures here, he said, were connected to rock structures near his home and to rock structures on Beaver Island in some large-scale grid network once set up by the Ancients.
>
> I told him we were working with the underwater structures in Rock Lake. Before I could continue, he interrupted as if to assure me that his stories were accurate and as if to test them himself. He had never seen the maps we had just produced of some of the structures. "The stone structures or buildings," he said, "are next to an ancient river or lake that over the years rose higher and higher until it was all under water. This was the Temple of the Moon, or Lake of the Moon. Nearby, there has to be a sign of an underwater panther."

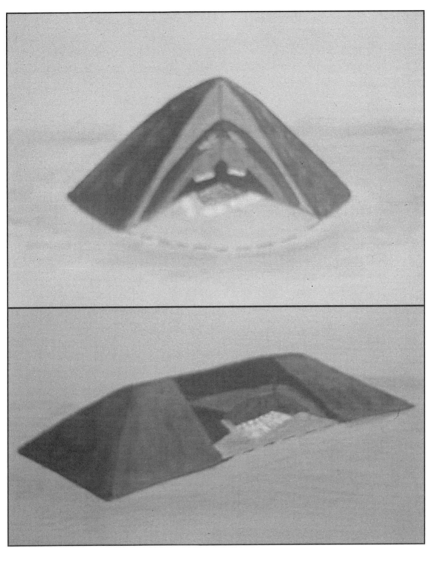

Conjectured interiors of one of Rock Lake's sunken mounds, based on identical pyramidal sites excavated at Cahokia. Left, alternating layers of lime plaster, stone, gravel, and clay form the internal structure built over a tomb containing copper weapons, mother-of-pearl beaded necklaces, and ceremonial objects of pink chert, surrounding a shallow grave containing the remains of a single individual, although burials of up to five persons have been found. These conical mounds belonged to royalty or shamans, society's elite. Below, Rock Lake's Limantis Pyramid features a similar interior design but conains the mass burial of dozens or possibly hundreds of individuals, members of the aristocracy.

I drew a sketch of Bass Rock Bar #1, which I have always thought similar in shape to the so-called panther mounds. He seemed satisfied. "Also," he said, "there must be a sign of a snake in that region. It is a snake that is shedding its skin (the ancient sign of rejuvenation or rebirth, as the growing snake discards its old skin and emerges in a clean, new one). This shedding snake is also the symbol associated with the moon, which goes through its phases again and again, month after month. Thus, the Place of the Moon could be read from the sign of the shedding snake."

I mentioned the dug out area on Eagle Island, which, when mapped, looks like a coiled snake chopped up. It also appears to have a plume or horn which I associated with Mexican symbols. It could hardly be from the time of the stone structures, though. I mentioned the one-third mile modified effigy east of Mud Lake, which, when mapped, also has the shape of a segmented or chopped up snake. He related this to a shedding snake and asked if there was a little spring or lake nearby. "Yes," I responded, "there is a dug out area near the head of this long snake, where water runs into Mud Lake, which, in turn, runs into Rock Lake." I have long suspected that if the large snake is partly man-modified, that the borough to modify it might have come from this depression, which also could have once been looked at as the source of the river that drained Rock Lake, one of the sources of the Crawfish River, and, therefore, the Rock River, a tributary of the Mississippi.

A Sacred Site

He said that near the snake the people (pilgrims) first came and offered sacrifices to the water there. The spot was religiously very important.

I offer the following data to support some of the privileged verbal history he was kind enough to share with me. For example, the stream that runs from Rock Lake goes into the Crawfish River, a tributary of Rock River. Except for some manmade rock fish-traps, there are not enough rocks in this river to warrant the name "Rock." I propose the possibility that the name "Rock River" comes from Rock Lake, which in turn was named for the numerous rocks on the bottom, which would have been above water circa 1500 B.C. Thus, the name may be very old indeed, as must the elder's oral tradition about the sunken Temple of the Moon, which relate to a time when the rock structures were above water. About 1500 B.C., lake levels in this region were some 30 to 40 feet below present.

That the famous Upper Mississippian cultural city of Aztalan is located along water routes a few miles from Rock Lake is, I believe,

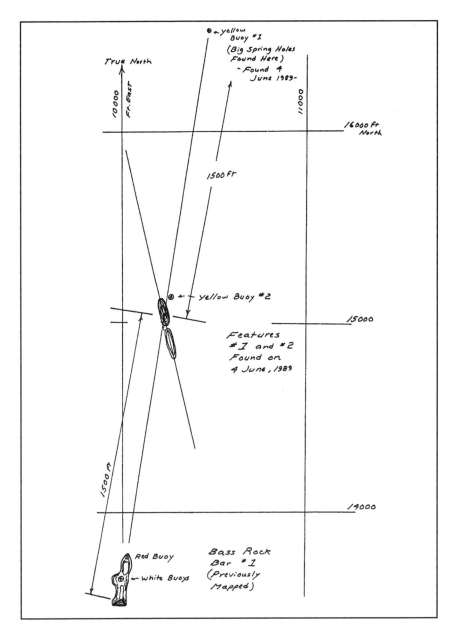

Dr. James Scherz's survey of the Rock Lake structures proves they were deliberately aligned to each other, thereby establishing their manmade origins. Bass Rock Bar No. 1, which is oriented true north, lies precisely 1,500 feet south of the Temple of the Moon, the Limnatis Pyramid (feature no. 1). In a straight line another 1,500 feet north are large holes for freshwater springs.

significant. The ceremonial center was long considered a northern outpost of this culture. Its presence in Wisconsin is unusual, in any case. Mounds across the river from Aztalan seem to form an integral part of the geometrical layout of the site, although they are much older than those behind the enclosure. There is a cultural continuity which hints at an important area that lingered for centuries in the minds of the native people. A model for this type of attachment might be Jerusalem in the Holy Land.

Mammoth earthworks heretofore not perceived nor considered appear around Rock Lake. These are giant, flat-topped mounds of the type found further south. Several modern houses around the lakeshore have been built on these structures. Such mounds are completely out of place in this region, unless it was once a very special spiritual center. Other data that should be considered are the giant rock fish-traps, rather unique to this area, north of Aztalan. Local collectors find arrowheads in their immediate proximity and residents have since pioneer days referred to them as "Indian fish weirs."

If we are considering a period sometime in the 16th century B.C. for the events which surrounded the structures in Rock Lake, we must take into account the economic climate of the region at the time. During this epoch, copper from Lake Superior was moving in astounding quantities between the waters of the Great Lakes and the Mississippi. Aztalan and Rock Lake could have comprised a trade support community along these commercial routes.

The Mexican-Wisconsin Connection

In Dr. Scherz's account of the Native American elder, the keeper of ancient oral traditions, reference was made to influences from Mesoamerica which extended as far north as Wisconsin and its foremost ceremonial center, Aztalan. There are numerous and intriguing cultural correspondences connecting North to Middle America in pre-Columbian times, suggesting that the Aztalaners and the Aztecs were indeed one and the same people.

Additional material evidence further bolsters this supposition, including the *atl-atl*, an Aztec term for "spear thrower." It was a kind of rigid sling or grooved stick with a hook at one end, which fitted the butt of the spear. Such an arrangement effectively lengthened the thrower's arm and propelled his missile at greater distances. It was frequently illustrated in Mixtec codices and appears on statues of Toltec warriors at Tula and Chichen Itza in Yucatan. The atl-atl was likewise the favorite weapon of the Aztalaners, who probably brought it with them from their Mexican homeland as they crossed into southern Wisconsin.

Similarities between Aztalan's temple mounds and leading features of Mexico City's Teotihuican are obvious enough. In either location, the structures are known as the Pyramid of the Moon and the Pyramid of the Sun, while the lunar monument at both sites is not only the smaller of the two but is positioned north of the solar pyramid.

The ancient architects of Aztalan laid a stone walkway just below the surface of a freshwater spring outside the city walls. Surviving oral traditions tell of another stone causeway that stretched out across Rock Lake to accommodate the shamans as they appeared to parade over the waters at night, a pair of torches held in their outstretched hands. Their performance was part of a prehistoric religious theater to awe the locals into superstitious submission. A similar walkway may still be seen as part of the Maya ceremonial road. Known as the Scabe, it follows the Yucatan shoreline just below the surface of the Caribbean for a quarter of a mile.[1]

It should be mentioned that roads deliberately constructed under water are not found outside coastal Mesoamerica and southern Wisconsin, so a relationship between these two areas would appear to be established by this infrequent cultural common denominator.

As James Kellar pointed out in his survey of North America's ancient stone mounds, several of which lie at the bottom of Rock Lake, the pyramidal monuments are tombs going back to the Adena period, beginning around the twelfth century B.C. It was from this epoch that an Ohio artifact was found which lent substantial credibility to North American contacts with Yucatan. The Waverly Tablet is a shaped, engraved stone which bears an uncanny resemblance to the Tablet of the Jester God, a Maya ceremonial object presently on display at Mexico City's famous Archaeological Museum.[2] Physical evidence such as this does indeed argue persuasively on behalf of Aztalaner origins in Middle America, or, at the very least, their close relationship with the kindred civilizations of the Toltecs and the Mayas.

Dr. Scherz's Indian contact also mentioned the Chinetec, a very old native American reference to Chinese mariners, who voyaged to these shores probably during the T'ang Dynasty, about 1,300 years ago. While Chinese influences in prehistoric America certainly existed, they are beyond the parameters of our investigation, which primarily include the early European Bronze Age or Atlantean and later Mesoamerican forces that impacted southern Wisconsin. Readers interested in learning about the Chinese sailors who visited America in prehistoric times are urged to seek out Gunnar Thompson's *Nu Sun,* by far the best book on the subject, thoroughly documented and eminently convincing.[3]

The mysteries of Rock Lake and the land its dynamic civilizers dominated have yet to be exhausted. They beckon to us still. We have solved some of them through the painstaking research of scientific inquiry—archaeology, anthropology, comparative mythology, geology. These methods have taken us thus far in a quest for reclaiming our country's hidden past. Now we shall use other methods, not of the dispassionate intellect, but of the visionary spirit, to recall into focus the echoes and shadows of times long ago, yet somehow strangely alive. They are far more than prehistorical curiosities. They comprise our national heritage.

Where purely scientific examination is no longer able to proceed, intuitive inspiration begins. One is the natural outgrowth of the other; they are complementary, like the two different hemispheres of the human brain. Science has shown us tantalizing fragments of a picture we want to behold in its entirety. So far, we have investigated the remnants of a dead civilization. Now we conjure its people back to life once more. Its material existence is gone, save for some telltale remains. But its spirit is alive. What has been denied us by coldly rational means shall be granted us by controlled dreaming. It is our door to the other world. Let us pass through it to experience wonders unseen for more than ten centuries.

·10·

Paranormal Occurrences

There are some secrets which do not permit themselves to be told.

—*Edgar Allen Poe*
"The Man in the Crowd"

A man in his early 40s climbed to the top of Aztalan's second largest temple mound early one autumnal evening. He was among the post-World War II archaeologists investigating the ancient earthwork's possible relationship to the positions of the moon, after which it had been named, an oral tradition handed down by the Winnebago. They were the last of the historic tribes to occupy southern Wisconsin.

Generally respected for his inquiring intelligence and community-oriented personality, the middle-aged researcher was himself a local resident with a background in surveying. He was joined after sundown by two colleagues, but the cold night air eventually made them return to the warmer comforts of home. He was determined to complete his observations, they said, but promised to join them shortly after midnight. They both reported that he was in good spirits before they left him around ten o'clock. But when morning came, he had not yet returned home, and his neighbors, having heard of his night vigil, searched for him in the achaeological zone. They found him still sitting atop the earthen pyramid, his hair and clothes in disarray. He barely acknowledged their presence, mumbled in meaningless sentence fragments, and stared wide-eyed, as though gazing on some horror his friends could not see.

The Lake Mills physician diagnosed his condition as "incoherent dementia," the result of shock, and he was sent to a Milwaukee clinic for observation. His treatment there having failed, he was transferred to an asylum in northern Wisconsin, where he died twelve years later. He was never able to tell anyone what happened that night he spent alone on Aztalan's Pyramid of the Moon. But his traumatic experience was the first occurrence of its kind known to have taken place in the Rock Lake area.

Interestingly, mental disorders are associated with the moon in cultures around the world, and many of these same cultures regard lunar phenomena as synonymous with psychic experience. The temple mound on which the unfortunate investigator spent that fateful might was, seven hundred years before, a ceremonial crematorium, in which the remains of ten shamans were interred. What was it about that prehistoric monument that was able to unhinge the mind of a man who, up until that night, never evidenced any sign of emotional disability?

Spirit of the Beaded Princess
More frequently, less troubling phenomena have been associated with Rock Lake/Aztalan. In 1991, a man was meditating near the burial mound of the Beaded Princess. The five-foot-high earthwork is located only a short distance north of the pyramidal city's walled enclosure and is presently situated on the grounds of the local museum.

When the mound was excavated in 1911, archaeologists from the Milwaukee County Museum were surprised to find the most fabulous tomb north of the Rio Grande. It contained the remains of a woman in her mid-twenties who had been interred wearing a gown decorated with nearly two thousand cut and polished mother-of-pearl beads arranged in three separate belts around her shoulders, waist, and ankles. Her real identity was unknown, but her high status among the ancient inhabitants of Aztalan could not be doubted.

Researchers generally concur that she was most likely a powerful medicine woman, or shaman, what we would refer to these days as a psychic, who was, however, taken far more seriously by her society than such persons are usually regarded in ours. For a people who strove to live in harmony with the observable patterns and cycles of Nature, as the Aztalaners did, according to the numerous astronomi-

Winter aerial perspective of the Pyramid of the Moon, Aztalan

cal alignments featured at their temple mounds, the shaman was their living connection to the will of heaven. And the more competent the medicine man or woman was in relating that will to the community, the greater they were honored—in life and after death. Hence, the elaborate burial of the Beaded Princess implies a person of very special influence.

It was at her mound that the man had come alone to quiet the turmoil of his mind and to seek the inner peace such sacred sites seem to radiate for receptive individuals. He thought of the woman buried at this place seven centuries ago, wondering who she might have been and feeling somewhat melancholy to realize that her skeleton and its splendid beadwork had been plundered by the archaeologists.

As these thoughts occupied his mind, a white bird suddenly landed atop the Beaded Princess mound and stared at him. He had never seen an albino robin before, but its abrupt appearance generated an unsettling sensation, some nameless emotion in his heart. The lovely white bird lingered as the man gradually began to feel a certain presence bordering on a sense of awe. Remembering his camera, he snapped a single photograph of the feathery apparition before it

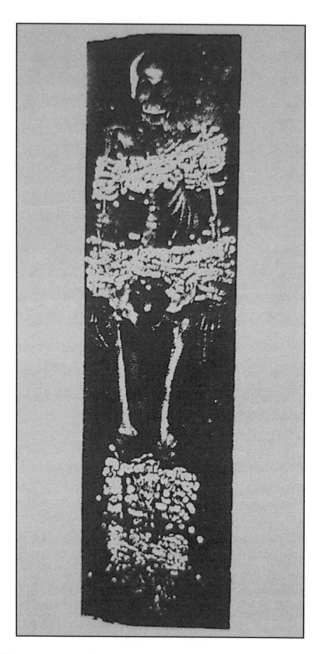

For exhibition purposes, the three belts of shells were removed from the remains of Aztalan's "Beaded Princess" by curators at the Milwaukee Public Museum and placed on a modern, better-preserved male *skeleton. Since its release in 1911, this photograph is still generally and incorrectly believed to portray the Princess.*

The real "Beaded Princess" at the moment of her discovery. Controversy still rages over her whereabouts, especially since officials at the Milwaukee Public Museum substituted the bones of a modern male for hers. While her skeleton is supposedly inventoried at the museum, some researchers believe it was never removed from her burial mound, where it still reposes.

flew away, never to be seen again. Its occurrence took place the same moment he was musing over the modern plight of the Beaded Princess. Was the albino robin atop the burial mound her spirit? While the appearance of the strange bird at Aztalan may seem trifling in this brief retelling, it was a deeply felt experience for its observer, who, as a consequence, was given a fuller appreciation of the site and its poetic, magical quality.

The Dark Side of Aztalan

Aztalan is still a powerful sacred center, because human activity, both good and evil, impacted the very ground and resonates today in the numinous landscape. Originally, the Aztalaners honored Father Sky by striving to live in tune with the observable changes of his sun, moon, and stars. Mother Earth showed her reciprocal gratitude by bringing forth harvests in abundance. Centuries of synchronous social behavior within the rhythm of nature imparted itself to the land. The temple mounds were deliberately and psychically engineered to concentrate telluric energies for spiritual empowerment, with which they radiate, undiminished by time, to this day.

But sometime around the beginning of the fourteenth century, Aztalan society fell into decline. Some of its inhabitants degenerated into ritual murder and even cannibalism, behavior that generated traumatic emotions, which likewise seeped into the immediate environment, charging it with a powerful negativity. It is this psychic dichotomy that prevails still at Aztalan, as evident in the diverse human activity its precinct continues to elicit. Wedding ceremonies take place every year atop the greater temple mound known as the Pyramid of the Sun. It was here, after A.D. 1100, that a sacred observatory stood to mark various positions of the rising sun, most particularly the winter solstice, and later became the focus of bloody sacrifices on behalf of a more pitiless solar god.

Those sacrifices still take place. During the summer of 1988, we found the remains of a small animal that had been ritually killed and placed in the center of a pentagon at the summit of the Pyramid of the Sun. In subsequent months, we occasionally came across weird symbols we recognized as the occult trademarks of Satanism spray-painted white near the Pyramid of the Moon. In time, we even got to meet a pair of Satanists from nearby Madison, who sometimes used the Aztalan enclosure for their ceremonies. One of them, an ordinary looking middle-aged man, exuded such a palpable aura of evil, we

Winter aerial view of Aztalan's Pyramid of the Sun

could not get away from him fast enough. His friend resembled an animated cadaver, a pale, scrawny wisp of a man, who spoke in a low, somewhat whistling voice. While such characters are not at all common at Aztalan, they do infrequently visit the ancient precinct for ritual activity, almost invariably after twilight. I include mention of them here as examples of the negative energy still vibrant behind the walls of Aztalan.

Ancient Power of Place

On the positive side, the Pyramid of the Moon has long been regarded as a place of rendezvous for lovers, who feel at once sheltered and exalted by close proximity to the smaller temple mound. Appropriately, the moon, from ancient times, was considered synonymous with eroticism.

But what is it about such a place that can so affect human behavior even today, for both good and evil, after so many centuries? Investigators of the paranormal believe answers to these questions lie in the very landscape of Aztalan. They insist its once formidable walls enclosed a sacred site, a place specifically chosen by geomancers, or shamans who interpreted the environment, for its spiritual qualities. These might include particular earth energies for healing, enhancement of psychic abilities, or astrological considerations. Nor were these prehistoric concepts so much archaic superstition.

Environmental scientists, such as James Lovelock, in his famous *Gaia Hypothesis*, now recognize Earth, not as an inanimate globe of dead matter whirling through space to no purpose, but as a biosphere of complex, organic interrelationships. Modern materialistic man does both his planet and himself an unspeakable disservice by arrogantly assuming he stands aloof from the living Earth.

The people who settled Aztalan attempted to balance their society according to the equipoise of the Cosmos, and in so doing they were far more keenly aware of telluric nuances in their surroundings. In fact, a heightened receptivity was part of their survival in the wild. Such a people, or, at any rate, its spiritual leaders, not only read the environment; they modified it, both deliberately and unintentionally. The magic they used was no lingering legerdemain, but a lost art of psychic manipulation of resident vibrations in natural and manmade surroundings. Places thus purposefully influenced, no matter how long ago, have their own mood, atmosphere, milieu, or feeling.

A case in point is the Topkapi Palace, in Istanbul, Turkey: "There are certain buildings that have drunk in so much of life about them that they are no longer mere structures of stone or wood, but rather stilled organisms that have captured the past, solidified it and hold it for the present."[1] What holds true for such buildings as Topkapi might be just as appropriately applied to Rock Lake and Aztalan. At the former location, the so-called "monster," reported there since the mid-1800s and memorialized in coastal effigy mounds at least six centuries before by the prehistoric natives, is still regarded by Oneida Indians as a "spirit guardian" conjured there by the ancient shamans to protect the sunken tombs of their honored dead from desecration.[2] No other explanation seems to account for the strong sensation of being watched that divers still experience in Rock Lake.

Terror Below
I have experienced it myself often enough. My first scuba dive took place when I was seventeen years old. Since then, I have participated in night dives into hazardous quarries, bubbled among barracuda off the coast of Yucatan, dove to the base of a volcano in the Atlantic Ocean, and other subsurface adventures. Never in any of these dives

was I afraid (perhaps unwisely). But years before I had heard stories of the Monster of Rock Lake or any spirit guardian there, I almost invariably felt uncomfortable in its depths to the point of dread. Nor was I alone. Virtually all the divers I knew honest enough to admit it told me they were "uneasy" for some reason in Rock Lake.

Only ninety feet at its deepest point (in the center of the northern half), with no treacherous currents, aggressive marine life, or dangerous obstructions, Rock Lake is threatening only for the thoughtless motorboat pilots who ignore our red and white "Diver Below!" flags. Certainly, that uneasiness scuba divers have known intensifies into terror when the bright green they glide through down to about thirty feet ends in a definable line, the thermocline, which separates the warm, upper temperatures from the much colder level below.

On the other side of the thermocline is some of the darkest, coldest water I have ever experienced. The darkness is so thick, an underwater lantern is able to project only a sharply delineated shaft of light, like a spotlight, illuminating what it directly falls upon and nothing else. It is down there, in that frigid, almost impenetrable blackness, where divers sense death all around them and feel they are under the hostile surveillance of some unseen entity lurking in the lightless, sacred realm through which they trespass. The feeling is often so strong, some divers never return to the lake after a single experience.

Even the shoreline, always lovely, likewise has its otherworldly moments. Long-time residents walking along the south end of the lake are sometimes inexplicably seized by a sudden dread. A young diver, a fellow townsman, confided to me that the lake, for all its beauty, always gave him "the creeps," both above and below the surface. A professional photographer who made several flights over Rock Lake in a rental plane from nearby Watertown Airport in the late 1980s shot dozens of 35mm rolls in an effort to capture the underwater structures on film. His slides of the subsurface delta or triangular platform at the southern end of the lake were the finest photographs ever taken of that elusive feature. Some years later, he burned every copy of this aerial discovery, offering no explanation, save that his actions were for purely personal reasons he could not disclose.

An Aura of Disorientation
Fear is not the only human response to the powers still operating at Rock Lake and Aztalan. In the mid-1980s, when teams of organized surveyors were attempting to obtain precise measurements of the

walled enclosure, many of the young people, mostly students from the University of Wisconsin (Madison), suffered nausea and disorientation. Even their instruments behaved erratically and malfunctioned. These unexpected symptoms occurred to a greater or lesser degree whenever different groups of students returned to Aztalan.

Sudden disorientation and mysterious equipment failures were similarly known to my own teams of researchers. No matter how thorough were our preparations before each expedition to Rock Lake, we experienced unusually high rates of engine malfunction aboard our boats, regardless of the craft we used. Two-way radios that had checked out perfectly at home refused to operate near Aztalan.

In the summer of 1989, I saw four expert scuba divers, one a master diver, another an open-water instructor, veer radically off a simple, straight-line compass bearing. They experienced under water the same disorientation the surveyors felt at Aztalan.

I cannot count the number of times outboard motors and chain saws (which were used to cut through the ice for winter dives, etc.) failed to operate whenever we brought them to Rock Lake. The instances of mechanical failure were so frequent and repetitive, we used to laugh, "The spirit guardian doesn't want us to find its pyramids!" We might have been more right than we realized at the time.

Perhaps most mysterious of all, these mechanical and mental aberrations occurred only when we were actively engaged in onsite research. Otherwise, human disorientation and instrument anomalies are no more frequent around Rock Lake and Aztalan than anywhere else.

My own first experience with the psychic side of Rock Lake took place in the winter of 1988. I was tired of hauling our equipment from my car on the deserted beach by sled over the ice cap, so I drove my new Honda across the solid surface to our position out over the middle of the lake. My decision was impulsive. I had never considered driving my car on the ice, nor ever discussed the possibility with anyone. Although I knew the nearly two-foot-thick surface was strong enough to support the car, it was a somewhat anxious trip across the same lake I had swum in only five months before.

I parked beside our research station and began unloading tools and instruments. At precisely 1:15, however, I was suddenly overcome by a terrible dread. I glanced at my watch, then the Honda, and envisioned it breaking through the ice, plunging into the lake below. I jumped into the front seat, gunned the engine, and sped back to shore.

The ice never showed any sign of cracking, and no doubt I could have left the vehicle safely out on the lake all winter. My silly anxiety had simply gotten the best of my nerves, I thought.

But when I arrived home, I learned that my mother, returning from shopping at exactly 1:15, had been abruptly seized with a nameless fear, as she envisioned my Honda crashing through the ice into the depths of Rock Lake. Had the lake acted as a psychic capacitor, magnifying my anxiety and sending it to someone 150 miles away, or was my subconscious alerted to the angry intentions of the spirit guardian below, to sink the trespasser's intruding car?

Mask Squeeze

Impressed by the unexpected psychic connection, I arranged a controlled experiment with my mother the following weekend when I returned to Wisconsin. At a prearranged time, she was to clear her mind while I would try to mentally send her a single image over the distance that separated us. When the moment arrived, I concentrated on a silver ring or circle, hoping this simple construct would be most easily received. At the prescribed time, however, what my mother received was not the pleasant image of a silver ring. Instead, the center of her forehead suddenly developed a spot of intense pain which spread in two straight lines down into her eyes and linked across the bridge of her nose, forming an agonizing triangle or pyramid outline. Had some other consciousness intruded into our mental telepathy to send us a warning? In any case, I resolved to permanently discontinue such experiments.

The following summer, we resumed our underwater exploration of Rock Lake. With us was John Shulak, the seventeen-year-old son of Richard, pilot of the *Mustard Seed*, which dropped anchor near a gargantuan stone monument just discovered by our sonar. The father stayed in the boat while John joined me in the water. Despite his youth, he was a competent diver. Even so, I was especially attentive to his gear and behavior during our slow descent. Everything checked out properly, and we were perhaps only a minute away from seeing the long-sought pyramid at sixty feet below when John showed signs of distress. We aborted the dive at once. At the surface, he tore off his mask, revealing a face disfigured by pain. His eyes were horribly swollen and ringed by thick, black circles. He was hauled into the boat, where he pressed two cold pop cans against his burning eyes. For long moments, he could not see. Only gradually his sight returned, although his vision was blurred and painful the rest of the day. All the tiny blood vessels around and in his eyes were ruptured. Had he remained submerged but a few seconds longer he might have suffered permanent damage and blindness.

His had been the most severe case of "mask squeeze" I had ever seen, a condition that results when a diver fails to equalize the outside pressure of his sinuses. Yet John insisted he had equalized properly, and I observed him do so regularly during our proper descent. Was he forbidden, as some suggested at the time, from beholding the sunken tomb by forces which had nothing in common with standard diving practices? John went down to see the pyramid but returned from it blinded. What karmic implications prevented him from seeing the long-lost Temple of the Moon? I thought back to the mental pyramidal outline that struck my mother's eyes the winter before. Maybe it had been a warning after all.

A Psychic Connection
My most recent telepathic experience at Rock Lake was unintentional but proved again (at least to my own satisfaction) the validity of such phenomena. I had just completed a rewarding day of extensive dives with my colleagues in the late spring of 1991. The weather and underwater conditions were glorious, and I got a good look at some intriguing sights about thirty feet down. Personal exhilaration of the sport had been enhanced with a sense of accomplishment. Later, I ate lunch alone in the park at the beach on the east side of the lake, while kids were splashing gleefully among the gentle waves. I still felt refreshed and exalted by that day's diving experience, but totally relaxed, and I imagined life could not possibly be more satisfying. The inner vibrations of my being seemed to hum in synchronicity with the rhythm of my pleasant surroundings. My thoughts were busied only with the afternoon sunshine glistening on the water through the trees. The world had slowed to a peaceful pace.

Into this tranquil if receptive frame of mind, a feeling of nameless urgency suddenly stabbed at my abdomen, followed immediately thereafter by the disturbing mental image of someone whose right hand had been amputated. It was as though this ghastly picture had been projected into my mind from an outside source. I certainly had not encouraged such an unsettling thought in my idyllic circumstances. I glanced nervously at my watch, then drove nonstop to my home in south suburban Chicago. As soon as I arrived there, I was told that my younger sister in southern Illinois had been seriously injured in a fall. The wrist of her right hand was shattered, she was in excruciating pain, and the doctors were not sure she would ever be able to regain the full use of her hand. I learned she fell at the same moment I glanced at my watch near the shore of Rock Lake, 450 miles away.

The thrill in recognizing this telepathic incident was at once marred by deep concern for my injured sister and my apparent inability to have helped her. After all, what good was such telepathy, if I could not use it to help? Perhaps, in prehistory, people knew how to employ their innate powers, and my experience represented only a useless remnant of what we all once possessed but have since lost.

A wise friend told me that I was wrong, that the instinctual response to my sister's distress over the hundreds of miles which separated us was itself an act of healing, wherein my brotherly spirit flew to assist her on levels physical and more than physical. My friend may have been right, because my sister, against the worst prognostications of her doctors, eventually regained almost total use of her injured wrist.

If I cast my mind back to that day when she fell, I am certain that my close proximity to Rock Lake at the time played a fundamental part in my telepathic experience. If so, then the lake's reputation for malevolence is not entirely deserved. I cannot shake the feeling that it acted like a gigantic reflector, a psychic amplifier or receiver, that picked up my sister's faraway pain and broadcast it to me in an image my conscious mind interpreted as an amputation. Certainly, my sister was in danger of losing her hand.

A Chicago Seer

Paranormal events at Rock Lake move not only laterally in time through the present, but backwards and forwards into the past and future. A case in point was my visit to Joseph DeLouise, a leading, well-known psychic, in 1988. As I walked through the door of his office in downtown Chicago with a bag of stones from the bottom of Rock Lake in my hands, he blurted out, "Why are you bringing me all those Indian stones?"

He could not have seen what was concealed in the bag and I had not mentioned the purpose of my visit, so his reaction at once established his credibility in my eyes. Even so, I told him nothing about our investigations of prehistoric Wisconsin.

DeLouise slipped into a light trance, and I put the manmade brick from one of the collapsed underwater pyramids into his hand. His reaction was immediate and violent.

"Oh," he started, and jerked his hand away from the artifact, as though it were suddenly too hot to touch. "There's blood on this stone! Somebody has been killed on it. No, they were murdered! I can see it was a young man. He was forced to kneel down, with his hands tied behind his back. Someone standing over him bashed his skull in with a stone axe, like this—!" And DeLouise made a chopping gesture with his right hand.

It was remarkable that he should have described such bloody activity associated with this stone, because historians believe human sacrifice took place at Rock Lake/Aztalan, but even more so because he was told absolutely nothing about the stone, where it came from, or the circumstances of its origin. There was nothing about it to indicate anything out of the ordinary.

When presented with a map of Rock Lake, DeLouise indicated two areas where the sunken monuments would be most easily found. During our next dive, we searched those areas thoroughly, finding nothing but weeds and mud. Only three years later did we realize he was right, when we discovered a line of five chimney-like features along the edge of the drop-off, about twenty feet below the surface. Our initial failure to find them just where DeLouise said we would had been caused by the thick silt layer which hid them from view, until a fortuitous temperature inversion in late summer 1991 cleared away the obscuring cover.

Casting his extraordinary inner vision into the immediate future, he said we would be offered a kind of "underwater sled" with which to explore Rock Lake.

"Do you mean a submarine or a tow bar pulled by a boat on the surface?" I asked. Knowing nothing of scuba equipment, he could not otherwise describe what he saw being made available for our efforts, except to say it was a self-propelled device too small for a submarine but nonetheless similar to one.

I did not know what he was talking about and put his strange prediction out of my head until some six months later, when I was discussing our Rock Lake investigations with some interested guests at the Lake Mills Fargo Mansion. A man entered in the course of our discussion and introduced himself as a resident of the town who had heard of our underwater research and offered his services as a diver.

"Have you ever used a scuba-scooter?" he asked. "Well, I've got two of them, and they're at your disposal, if you think you can use them."

A scuba-scooter is no more than an electric motor encased in a streamlined cowling and powering a single fan-like propeller. It is attached to a pair of handles, which a diver grasps as it pulls him through the water like a submersible sled. It was the very device Joseph DeLouise had predicted we would be offered.

His mind ranged with ease from the future back into the past. He described the ancient Aztalaners' physical appearance: "They're not regular Indians, but they're not Europeans, either. They're pretty tall, with long, dark hair, but fairer skin than Indians and less bony facial features. Many of them have light eyes—gray, hazel, light brown."

He saw a time of betrayal and mass violence, which ultimately led to the downfall of Aztalan and the incineration of its walls. Much of what he said was confirmed or at least suggested by Wisconsin's archaeological record, which, of course, he had never studied. After several sessions with DeLouise, any rational, open-minded person would have concluded that his "readings" were valid.

While enlightening, I also found such time-traversing observations disturbing, because they undermined my preconceived understanding of the future. Nothing can be predicted, I thought, because the future does not yet exist. Yet DeLouise's accurate precognition threw that supposition into question. I still do not have the answer.

The Temperamental Spirit-Guardian

Nor were there answers for the numerous equipment breakdowns experienced at the upper Midwest's foremost sacred site. A recent example of mechanical failure occurred in spring 1992, when a team of five divers, archaeologists, and anthropologists from the University of Wisconsin at Madison accompanied me on a search for the monument discovered the previous autumn. They brought along a huge underwater camera, a costly and sophisticated affair used by professional oceanographers and something out of the undersea adventures of Jacques Cousteau. Its operator was highly skilled in its use and performed all the standard pre-dive checks.

No sooner had it been lowered into the lake than it flooded—"an impossibility," according to the mortified photographer. Its inexplicable failure was the prelude to an unusual dive. Subsurface visibility was poor, as usual, and I had difficulty even relocating the drop-off, where the chimney-like towers stood in a curving line. My professionally trained guests had asked me to show them a stone pyramid, even though they were very skeptical of such a structure actually existing on the bottom. Their attitude was more challenging than supportive.

Despite the turbid conditions and ten-foot visibility, I was able to locate one of the mysterious stone circles, and they were surprised that the phenomenon really did exist after all. But just as their interest began to spark, a powerful wind suddenly arose from the south to blow a thick mass of green algae across the face of the waters. A heavy curtain was being drawn over the sunken monuments.

It was as though the guardian spirit of Rock Lake had decreed, "All right, you doubters! You refuse to believe such things as my drowned city of the dead are possible. Here is a brief look to change your minds, but you do not deserve to see any more than this glimpse!"

The persistent failure of equipment and recurring instrument anomalies at Rock Lake have their origins, some believe, in a tragedy that happened before the Civil War, when a farmer was building his house on a hill just west of the shore. By mid-winter, the surface froze over sufficiently to create an ice cap more than a foot thick, so the farmer used it to save time hauling building materials from the east. He hitched his team of four horses up to a wagon full of bricks and drove straight across the lake to his construction site past the opposite shore.

The shortcut did indeed save time, but he grew ambitious and began expanding the original plans for his home. Deliveries of stone continued through the winter and into early spring, when the first thaw took place. In early March, he drove across the still-frozen surface with yet another load, despite ominous puddles of water on the ice.

He was out about halfway when the ice suddenly broke open. In the space of a few seconds, the wagonload of bricks, its hapless team of horses, and the driver all plunged to the bottom of Rock Lake.[3]

Winnebago still residing in the area believed the farmer had been punished by the spirit guardian for his greed.

August Derleth, regional author who founded Arkham House Publishers to preserve the stories of horror writer H.P. Lovecraft, wrote that southern Wisconsin was the weirdest stretch of territory in North America. Stranger things happen there, he insisted, than just about anywhere else in the country. The mystery belongs to the very landscape, beautiful as it certainly is, which somehow draws into itself bizarre and sometimes bloody human behavior.

We think of Jeffrey Dahmer, whose murderous career in Milwaukee was a hideous mirror-image of the ritual sacrifices that went on behind the walls of Aztalan, only an hour's drive away in space but seven hundred years ago in time. Is there something inherent in the very environment of southern Wisconsin that still influences us?

The Disappearing Stone

Lois Zimmerman and her husband are lifelong Lake Mills residents who have a home near the south shore of Rock Lake. Over the years, they have noticed a peculiar occurrence no one has been able to explain.

It does not happen regularly, nor even annually, but has taken place at different intervals perhaps a dozen times during the last twenty years. The Zimmermans have seen a large, although otherwise unremarkable, boulder appear above the surface of the water, usually less than a hundred feet out into the lake, at a position they know a rock of such size should not exist.

The anomalous feature will be visible for a day or so, then vanish. Attempts to locate it in the shallow, decidedly un-stony waters off Sandy Beach invariably fail. The Zimmermans noticed that lake levels always remained unchanged before, during, and after the boulder's brief appearance, an observation confirmed by monitors from the Department of Natural Resources.

Other residents at the south end of Rock Lake have witnessed the same phenomenon. An Oneida Indian shaman laughed when he heard about the Zimmermans' disappearing rock.

"They better not bring it into their house! It is a spirit stone, which goes into and out of what you call 'dimensions.' Anyone who has it in their possession may be taken along, backward or forward in time, or to the spirit world. The stone appears and goes away to warn people that Tyranena is a sacred lake."

The shaman later went to Missouri Hill, where he recognized the arrangement of its stones as typifying the Bear Clan. These were ferocious fighters, he explained, who acted as constables to protect the ancient residents of Rock Lake and Aztalan from the surrounding tribes of less sophisticated natives.

Missouri Hill was a place of initiation and spiritual training, a kind of occult police academy, where healing techniques were also taught, as part of the bear's symbolism (i.e., its regenerative powers, as implicit in the creature's long, death-like hibernation, from which it emerges refreshed).

A great many extraordinary occurrences associated with Rock Lake and Aztalan have been reported over the years. Those described here represent only a fraction of a much larger collection. Together, varied as they are, they underscore the general feeling that Rock Lake is far more than a recreational park, no different from hundreds of others throughout Wisconsin. As the Oneida shaman said, "it is a sacred lake."

·11·

Psychics at
the Sacred Center

*This is the place. Stand still. Let me review the scene and
summon from the shadowy past the forms that once have been.*
—Longfellow

I had been impressed enough with the work of Joseph DeLouise to
pursue a psychic line of research at Rock Lake and Aztalan, but I
hesitated until I could find adepts who seemed uniquely receptive
to the singular energies manifest at these ancient sites. My reluctance
paid off, because three women of exceptional insight found their way
to our ongoing inquiry: Lorraine Darr of Iowa, Marene Martensen in
Milwaukee, and Linda Horacek from Illinois.

Lorraine was already well known to me through her pronouncements on the crystal skull, the Atlanto-Mayan sculpture of a human
female skull carved from solid quartz crystal. I met her for the first
time under memorable circumstances.

My colleagues and I planned a big Halloween weekend at Rock
Lake, with a two-man submarine and camera crews from the Fox
television network. Practically at the last moment, everything fell
through and, instead of a major investigation, I could find neither a
boat to take me out nor even one other diver to accompany me. The
situation was made all the more frustrating by the unusually clear visibility of the water. Throughout 1992, from spring to fall, we had not

had a single productive dive because of the subsurface turbidity. Now the lake was opening up, soon to close again, as the cold weather began to descend on Wisconsin. October 31st would be our last opportunity for a dive until at least the following spring.

Discovery and Loss
Determined to make the most of it, I suited up in the cold but windless air and stepped off from the north shore at the edge of the wooded area known as Tyranena Park. The water was still relatively warm, but diving alone into a lake concealing a monstrous spirit guardian said to be protecting an ancient city of the dead can be a chilling experience, especially on Halloween. The sky was leaden with a dull overcast, and the surface of the lake was mirror smooth. Down below, despite the gloomy lighting conditions, I was very pleased to be able to see my way around through the twenty-foot visibility and made for the direction of Zeke's Wall. This was the name given to an artificial-looking rock pile glimpsed infrequently by fishermen since at least the turn of the last century. It was picked up on our sonar sweep of 1989 but so far had rarely been seen by divers.

I hoped the uncommonly fine clarity would make it possible for me to locate the elusive structure. Following my compass bearing according to the sonar chart, I maintained a southwesterly course, and in perhaps fifteen minutes found what I assumed was the target. It was indeed a large rock pile, unusual only because it was the only such assemblage on the otherwise muddy bottom.

The chaos of undressed stones had an entirely natural appearance reminiscent of the glacier that carved out Rock Lake twelve thousand years ago. But as I swam around the haphazard collection of lithic debris, escorted by some oversized and inquisitive bass, I spotted a feature that looked decidedly unnatural. Though in an extremely ruinous condition, enough of it still stood to present the most pyramidal structure so far encountered in the lake. It reared up from the bottom and fronted the south flank of the rock pile. The visible section, the upper portion not obscured by the silt, stood about five feet tall at a depth below the surface of less than twenty feet. While one side was in relatively good condition, the back (if that is what it was) had almost completely collapsed.

As often as I swam around and over the figure, I could not determine if it was essentially circular like the chimney targets we had located the previous year on the other side of the lake, but it was unquestionably manmade and more massive than the chimney-like structures lining the drop-off. Some of the stones at its base (or, at any rate, those visible through the silt) were quite large and must have weighed at least two hundred pounds apiece. The structure tapered from its broad, lower section to a genuine apex, although even in its best parts, many pieces appeared to be missing. The pyramid seemed at once powerful and fragile—as though, having endured for centuries in its watery tomb, it might collapse at any moment. Its obviously artificial character called into question the apparently natural rock pile it fronted. Was this Zeke's Wall and was it really a "wall"? Was it as manmade as the pyramidal structure, but more ruined? Perhaps the pyramid had been somehow related to it.

Although I nurtured my air well, I did not have time for these speculations; I reached around for my 35mm camera. I was glad that my ex-diving instructor, Doug Gossage, and I had thoroughly checked out its operation the night before and installed fresh batteries. It was in perfect working order and loaded with Kodak 1200, a grainy but high-speed film for shooting in conditions of low light. I centered the pyramid in the view finder and pushed the shutter button. Nothing happened. I re-examined the reliable Hanamax and did everything I could to make it function. It was dead.

I dropped the marker buoy, rose to the surface as quickly as I could, and swam for shore. Divesting myself only of my tank and fins, I drove at top speed, still in my dripping scuba outfit, back to Lloyd Hornbostel's house on the lake in the hope he had an underwater camera on hand. He did, although it was already loaded with only 400 ASA film. I was not sure it could capture the pyramid in the subsurface gloom. I raced back to Tyranena Park, threw on my tank and fins, launched myself into the water once more, swam for the marker buoy, dove to the structure at Zeke's Wall, got it in the view finder, and pressed the shutter button. It jammed, not at all to my surprise. After six consecutive years of diving in Rock Lake, I had come to expect as much.

I fought to unjam the mechanism; the visibility, earlier so clear, rapidly declined to little more than half its former transparency in the waning afternoon sunlight. I felt I was in a struggle with the lake, which had only tantalized me with a glimpse of an unknown pyramid and was now spoiling my best efforts to photograph it. At last, running low on air and under deteriorating light conditions, I freed up the shutter button and shot a whole roll of the structure. Several days later, the photos were developed. All but one were ruined by causes we were unable to determine with any certainty. Even the lone, unspoiled example was just barely passable. Several local people have told me it is as though the pyramids are trying to hide from anybody who tries to get a really good look at them.

Lorraine Darr

As I walked out of the water back toward shore, I thought to myself, "If a nineteenth-century Menomonie Indian were to see me now, he would think I was one of the Marine Men coming back for some copper."

As I made my way across the shore, I saw a woman in her sixties standing near the water. Assuming she was a Lake Mills resident, I asked her if she had ever had any unusual experiences at Rock Lake. "Not yet," she said, and went on to describe the magical quality of this serene sacred site. But as she spoke, I began to recognize her voice from our several telephone conversations. Thus transpired my introduction to Lorraine Darr, one of the leading psychics in the world today.

Notwithstanding her powerful insights, she is a naturally compassionate lady I came to trust and admire at once. Nationally known for her psychic pronouncements, she initiated a major phase of her own personal quest when she visited Egypt in 1983. After that transforming experience, her life as one of America's best-respected seers has made her sought after by researchers, and her "communications" have appeared in five books, including the well-known *Birth of a Modern Shaman* and *The Sedona Vortex Guidebook*. Her responses to my questions about Rock Lake and Aztalan were mostly "channeled," but of so mild and informal a character, they seemed to speak from her without effort or any effect on her.

Marene Martensen

Lorraine's friend and colleague, Marene Martensen, also loaned her talents to our investigation of southern Wisconsin's otherworld. She is uniquely qualified to speak for the spiritual energies of Aztalan because of her deep personal involvement there over the years. Since 1979, she has been powerfully drawn to the ancient enclosure, particularly to the Pyramid of the Moon. Its earthen temple mound was the scene for "the peak emotional experience" of her life, as she connected with the potent forces at work in the sacred center.

"The moon mound is my home," she says, because it constitutes "a fairy-like energy" like no other place. She has conducted four-hour-long ceremonies with eight other women initiates atop the pyramid for purposes of spiritual empowerment and personal growth. They

Lorraine Darr

meditated with crystals and the music of drums at the moment of a solar eclipse to conjure the feminine powers of the site. Most of her pilgrimages to Aztalan take place just before the new moon, a time of "letting go" and purgation.

Born in Chicago, Marene became a full-time healer and researcher in the paranormal field after she moved to Wisconsin. She has been a career psychic since 1977, and her nurturing professionalism continues to touch the lives of many persons in need of wholeness.

Marene Martensen

Linda Horacek
Hard put to find another psychic with the exemplary credentials of Lorraine and Marene, I was nevertheless fortunate enough to meet Linda Horacek, appropriately enough at a "psychic fair." Linda's outstanding talent in psychometry ideally qualified her for unlocking some of the mysteries associated with the artifacts of Rock Lake and Aztalan.

Psychometry is the ability some persons possess to receive impressions—visual, auditory, or otherwise—from an object they touch physically. Often such objects are imbued with the psychic residue of

Linda Horacek

past emotion or still resonate with traces of human contact, regardless of the passage of time.

Linda Horacek journeyed far from her home in suburban Chicago, when she followed a solitary quest into the high Andes of Peru and Bolivia. No ordinary tourist, she researched the temples and lost cities of the Incas and tapped her subconscious into the energies of a vanished people.

It was an uncommonly brave thing to do for a petite American blonde, traveling alone in a faraway country known for its dangers. But she was driven by a profound sense of destiny, which apparently shielded her and returned her to America fine-tuned for her life's work as a healer. Today a professional psychometrist, she has worked with legal departments and law enforcement agencies on missing-child and murder cases.

After graduating from George Williams College, Linda lectured at Northern Illinois University, hosted a television show about paranormal activities, and was a media producer and marketer for business people and their products. She presently heads up Horacek and Associates for personal consultations and is busy writing a new book about archangels. But it is her psychometric gifts which make her eminently qualified as a modern-day seer.

Different as they are in terms of age, origins, and backgrounds, it is interesting to observe that the three psychics each began their paranormal careers after having made some crucial trip to a site of outstanding spiritual power: Lorraine to Egypt's Great Pyramid, Marene to Aztalan's Pyramid of the Moon, and Linda to Tiahuanaco in the Andes, the ancient capital of a pre-Incan civilization.

Psychometry of the Artifacts

My intention in assembling these extraordinary women was to pool their special abilities by giving them opportunities to hold various artifacts pertaining to Rock Lake and Aztalan. I hoped they would be able to retrieve whatever memories might lie within the materials we collected during our research. It was a strange collection indeed. It comprised a calcite crystal, two bones, the old photograph of a skeleton, and three unremarkable stones.

All the items were picked up in the course of our numerous dives, save for the crystal, appropriately shaped like a pyramid; it even has what could pass for a little altar at its summit. It is, however, entirely natural, and was found along Rock Lake's northwestern shore about sixty years ago by a local resident.

The knuckle bone of a deer was found among the stones of a volcano-like structure in the southwest quadrant of the lake during our investigation of that structure in 1989. The other deer bone, a broken femur, was taken from a smaller platform mound in the north-central section. A stone still bearing traces of cement or plaster belonging to the Limnatis Pyramid, lying sixty feet beneath the surface, was included with a verified manmade brick from a conical pyramid collapsed off the eastern shore.

But the object that most intrigued me was a triangular, roughly wedge-shaped stone I found in September 1991, when Lloyd Hornbostel and I for the first time encountered the half-dozen annular stone monuments and cairns positioned along the drop-off in the west-central quadrant of the lake, about twenty feet down. I recall that the stone attracted my attention because it alone of all the others it lay among was not round. I vaguely remember prying it from the bottom, but I have no recollection of carrying the five-pound weight to the surface, nor of placing it in our boat. More remarkable, we much later noticed that the stone bore the apparent image of what appeared

*Objects taken from Rock Lake and psychometrized by our investigators:
a manmade brick, the ship stone, a small piece of the Temple of the Moon,
bones from two different pyramid sites, and a pyramidal calcite quartz*

to be a sailing ship from the ancient world. Although badly eroded, the relief-like figure is clearly discernible when direct light passes at right angles across it, highlighting the raised portion in shadow.

A contact-ink impression of the stone even more clearly revealed the outline of what looks like an ancient sailing ship, although laboratory tests using hydrochloric acid to determine its artificial identity were inconclusive. It was proposed to submerge the stone in a stronger acid solution that would burn away all the solidified accretion that covers the image. The acid bath would either reveal what lay underneath in an approximation of its original condition or melt the stone down to nothing. I refused to take that chance and turned to other means of establishing its real origins.

If the stone is somehow verified for what it appears to be—a manmade marker bearing the likeness of a merchant vessel from the ancient European world—it could be among the most dogma-shattering discoveries ever made, representing as it would material proof that visitors to prehistoric America arrived from the other side of the Atlantic Ocean. It would also prove that the underwater structures were indeed authentic ruins of a lost civilization. Beyond the provocative image itself, the indented crescent in which it seems to ride appears made for the purpose of accommodating the "ship." Moreover, the roughly pyramidal shape of the stone would make a suitable capstone or apex to any one of the monuments we have seen on the bottom of Rock Lake. The stone in question was, after all, found practically adjacent to a large, collapsed structure.

A Startling Comparison

Unable to positively establish its manmade identity through standard testing, I resigned myself to accepting the stone as a natural curiosity, a happy simulacrum, although I still felt a personal attachment to it. But while casually paging through the latest Numismatic Fine Arts Association catalog during the production of this book, I was amazed to find a virtually identical representation of the Rock Lake find. Number 130 in the catalog was a 17mm long stone seal from Israel dated to the ninth century B.C. On its face was the depiction of a maritime vessel which, detail for detail, was practically a duplicate of the craft suggested by the Rock Lake stone.

As the catalog explains, "This spectacular scaraboid offers the first realistic representation of a ship on a Hebrew seal, and the only ship in Jewish art datable to the First Temple period. This is hardly surprising, as the Hebrews were not a seafaring people, their coastline being largely inhabited by Phoenicians and Philistines. The ship depicted on this seal is apparently a merchant vessel designed for long sea voyages, rather than a war galley. It must have been based upon a real-life model, possibly one of the famous Tarsish ships built by Jehoshaphat, king of Judah from 867 to 846 B.C. (I Kings 22:49–50; II Chronicles 20:36–37). The design could indicate that the owner of the seal was a mariner or otherwise connected with the sea trade."[1]

Does the image on the Rock Lake stone belong to a Hebrew ship? And if so, are the structures at the bottom of the lake, by inference, likewise the works of ancient Hebrews? I thought back to the Gigals, conical piles or "heaps" of stone mentioned in the Old Testament. They were raised by the Hebrews to mark their crossing of the River Jordan into the Promised Land. Then there was Ohio's fifty-foot high stone mound that contained a tablet with Hebrew inscription.

But, as the N.F.A.A. catalog pointed out, "the Hebrews were not a seafaring people." The ship on the seal is not so much Hebrew as typical of the freighters in use by such diverse nationalities as the

Stone found in Rock Lake, possibly portraying the carved image of a sailing ship

*Eighth century B.C. stone seal from ancient Israel depicting a sailing
vessel similar to the craft appearing on the Rock Lake stone*

Etruscans, Iberians, and Phoenicians, who were probably hired by the Hebrews to engage in commerce. But the design was known long before the rise of the Levant's mercantile power, dating back to the Atlantean "Sea Peoples" of the Late Bronze Age.

In fact, the N.F.A.A. article mentions Tarshish in connection with the ship illustrated on the seal, a particularly cogent detail, because Tarshish, near the Atlantic coast of Andalusian Spain, its ruins covered by the modern town of Huelva, has been directly associated with Atlantis from Roman sources to modern scholars.[2] Elena Whishaw, a leading archaeologist in the 1920s, excavated abundant evidence for an Atlantean presence there, and Donald Lenzen, an expert in ancient weights and measures, supported her findings with the latest research.[3] Indeed, Tarshish (or Tartessos, as it was known in classical times) is generally assumed by investigators to have been the capital of Gadeiros, the Atlantean kingdom described by Plato as occupying the Atlantic coasts of Spain.[4]

Whether a Phoenician freighter owned by Hebrew investors or a merchantman from Atlantis, the seal should make us wonder if its twin appears on the Rock Lake stone, which may once have been part of a memorial to seafarers many centuries ago. In any case, the controversial stone, together with its companion pieces, provided ample evidence of a forgotten past now up to our psychics to uncover.

•12•

The Psychics
and the Artifacts

*One looks back with appreciation to the brilliant teachers, but
with gratitude to those who touched our human feelings.*
—*Carl Jung*

I was particularly interested to learn what our psychics had to say about my favorite underwater find. I placed it first in the hands of Lorraine Darr.

There was nothing melodramatic about her method of "accessing" the artifact. She only shut her eyes for a moment, took a breath, then spoke in a normal tone of voice as she described the impressions received from this curious discovery.

My own procedure was simple: to say virtually nothing about the objects, not to test Lorraine, Marene, and Linda, but to keep their focus uncluttered by any outside input that might unfairly influence their perceptions. Whatever they said had to come directly by way of their own abilities to "read" the artifact, untainted by external distractions.

Moreover, sessions for each psychic were separated by three states and several weeks, their readings were never held together in common, and there were no verbal or written communications between them for the duration of their work on this project. I did make something of an exception with Linda. Unlike Lorraine and Marene, she was not familiar with my previous book about Rock Lake, knew very little of our research there, and was told nothing about the objects, save that they came from a Wisconsin lake.

The Ship Stone

Whether or not the stone's image of a sailing vessel was actually sculpted by man or fortuitously fashioned by natural forces, Lorraine felt very strongly that it was associated with the early civilizers who voyaged to Rock Lake from very far away. They were proud of their great maritime achievement, which they regarded, she said, as "the Journey of Mankind." These ancient travelers did not blindly stray from their Atlantic homeland, but deliberately set out to map the entire surface of the globe, following what they perceived as linear patterns of earth energy, which belonged to a world grid or network of subterranean forces, some magnetic, mostly telluric, of the kind intuited by dowsers.

By properly reading those forces—either by way of some lost technology or via heightened psychic awareness or both—the "Diviners," as the seafarers were often known among their own and other peoples, were, in fact, similar to modern-day dowsers, who are able to find water, oil, and other underground targets, largely through a kind of intuition. So adept were the Diviners at reading these subterranean lines of flowing energy, that they could determine which led to deposits of certain minerals, subsurface freshwater springs, etc., by interpreting the particular variations or character of local energies.

Thus using their greatly expanded dowsing expertise, which they long ago perfected and elevated to a national science, they were guided along subterranean and undersea pathways across the planet, charting the world grid as they traveled to invisible crossroads, where the pathways intersected each other to form power points of focused energy. It was this understanding and application of the energy lines which brought the Diviners straight to Michigan's Upper Peninsula, the greatest copper deposit on earth, and directed them to settle around the shores of Rock Lake and on the banks of the Crawfish River at Aztalan. We recall that Dr. Scherz's Indian informant told of a similar energy network used by the ancients.

The lake is especially sacred for the underground rivers that converge directly below it, thereby creating a particularly strong concentration of earth energies, which the Diviners were able to transform into both mechanical and spiritual (psychic) powers.

Lorraine felt that a ship like that depicted on the wedge-shaped stone actually lies buried under a stone mound at the bottom of Rock Lake. It was intentionally placed there with a great deal of ceremonial solemnity, as a commemorative monument to the "Journey of Mankind," an accomplishment anciently regarded as the fulfillment of a high destiny. The entombed ship, Lorraine believes, still lying beneath Rock Lake, was put there to memorialize the Diviners' coming, because it was either the first or among the very first of their vessels to arrive in southern Wisconsin, around 3000 B.C.

The buried ship exists on several levels of simultaneous meaning, not only as a monument to the first people who voyaged to Wisconsin, but also as a symbol of the greater journey through life. The hull was a vessel in the same sense that the body is the vessel of the soul, as it carries both on the quest to human destiny. It likewise marks the place where "the True Flame" was re-established in the new land to "honor the gods and define the cross point of the chi, dragon power, or earth energies which meet there." The True Flame was one of several names by which the religion of the soul's rebirth or transmigration was known; hence, its serpent or "dragon" symbolism, particularly in the snake's ability to slough off its old skin for a new one, the bringing about of self-transformation.

Interestingly, the True Flame is a religion that originated in Atlantis, as did the early comers to Rock Lake, and was likewise described by Edgar Cayce, the "Sleeping Prophet," in several of his "life-readings" about the sunken civilization.[1] But neither Cayce nor Lorraine could have ever suspected the very real and valid historical basis for their coincidental vision of the True Flame cult. As mentioned in our chapter about Atlantis, the Lughnasadh was a sacred-fire religion practiced in pre-Christian Ireland, whence it was brought by Atlanteans known to Irish tradition as the Formorach.[2]

The same fire ritual occurred throughout the South and Midwest of prehistoric America, where even its name lost little of its Atlantean-Irish character: the Loughe. Paralleling the astronomical fixes at Aztalan's Pyramid of the Sun, oriented as it is to the winter solstice, both the pre-Christian Irish and pre-Columbian American rituals were likewise celebrated on the first day of winter. Lorraine's testimony about the True Flame comprises credible confirmation that what she "saw" taking place at Rock Lake thousands of years ago actually happened.

Marene Holds the Ship Stone

Marene's reading of the curious ship stone was remarkably similar in many details, save any mention of the True Flame cult. She saw a European-like people who traveled a great distance from a faraway place of origin, "which was very different from their landfall in the new country." The homeland they left behind was fertile but mountainous and sea-girt, its people naturally joyous and outgoing, although tending toward domination and exploitation. Culturally brilliant and physically courageous, they feared nothing and believed all things were possible.

She saw their ship (the one portrayed on the stone) escorted by birds as they drew away from their island home. The voyagers regarded their transoceanic voyage as a wonderful adventure. But they were deeply religious, making elaborate appeals for spiritual and material guidance to their many gods, before, while, and after they set sail. Their vessel was surrounded by "goddess energy," and Marene envisioned several accompanying crescent-moon insignia, as well as the emblem of a winged face—lunar symbols that coincided with Rock Lake's identity as the precinct for the Temple of the Moon, according to surviving native American tradition.

A string of related words flashed through Marene's consciousness: "Message stone, deliberately placed. Keystone. Figurehead. Sign. The name of the journey; its purpose. Hieroglyphic." They all seem to properly define the object in light of everything else we have learned about it and its surroundings. Her mention of "the name of the journey; its purpose" demonstrates just how closely she came to Lorraine's reading, which was separated from Marene's by fifty miles and five hours. The birds she noticed in association with the ship call to mind a navigational practice made aboard Bronze Age vessels and still employed by oceangoing Vikings as late at the tenth century A.D. Cages of birds were brought along as standard equipment to be used when the captain, far out to sea, needed to determine the nearest landfall. The ravens were let loose.Their black plumage made them stand out against the sky better than other birds. They rose circling over the ship, then flew straight for the closest dry land.[3]

Linda "Hears" the Ship Stone

Linda felt that the image on the stone was manmade and said tool marks might be found on its surface if the accretions were stripped away. She saw the stone being deliberately placed at a specific location, where it stood for a very long time. Thus set up "as a marker," it was intended to commemorate "some important exploration," and became the focus for "oaths" sworn by generations of lake dwellers to maintain their faith with the courage and vision of the first people who arrived in Wisconsin.

But the ship stone is not unique; other, similar examples lie far down below. She perceived "an underwater boat" still sunk far beneath the bottom of Rock Lake, just as Lorraine did. It was "an exploratory boat," preserved and memorialized as among the earliest such craft to reach the new land.

Linda envisioned a purplish blue fire intimately associated with the ship stone. Perhaps this was the True Flame symbol of the mystery cult practiced by the prehistoric inhabitants of the Midwest. She felt its warmth, which is the lingering energy infused into it by the Diviners. They used it for healing, particularly for the treatment of cancer and similar diseases. It possesses radiation properties of a very old kind Linda had not encountered before. For all its ancient usage, the purple fire still glowed with a salutary warmth available to persons, even today.

Interestingly, Linda experienced a fleeting moment of clairaudience when she briefly heard singing, more like chanting, in connection with the ship stone. Later, when Marene psychometrized a stone from one of the larger Rock Lake pyramids, she said its builders literally "enchanted" the structure through ritual singing. Cross references such as these tend to confirm the impressions of our sensitive investigators.

The Brick

As mentioned in a previous chapter, Joseph DeLouise, the Chicago psychic, received a shock from the brick I retrieved from the site of a collapsed conical pyramid about twenty feet below the surface of Rock Lake. He felt a murder had been associated with it.

Marene sensed a similar negativity, but regarded the human destructiveness of the past as a force of nature, like an earthquake. She began by envisioning alternating lines of light and darkness, from which stepped a tall figure, who spoke to her: "An ancient civilization that reverts to instinctual behavior will always rise again." The implication of these words, she felt, meant that Aztalan is undergoing a cycle of re-emergence, in which present renewed interest in Rock Lake is bringing the forgotten civilization back into general consciousness, at once fulfilling the destiny of the ancient Aztalaners and providing our time with the historical guidance we need to save our planet.

Marene felt the structure of which the brick was formerly a part belonged to a later period of tyrannical hierarchy, in which the old spirituality, while never extinguished, was nevertheless diminished by numerous acts of bloodshed, which stamped its violent energies into the sub-matrix of the brick itself.

Memories in Stone

Words also came to Lorraine, as she placed her hand on the artifact: "The stone itself holds memories." These, too, were of a negative kind. An outside people invaded the Rock Lake area. "They were brutally ignorant, at once fearful and jealous of the Diviners who built the beautiful monuments, and killed them because they were supposedly possessed by demons." Even some important visionaries perished in the chaos. Certainly, Wisconsin's ancient civilization came to a disastrous end not planned for it by its founders.

Linda correctly identified the brick as originally "part of a larger work. It was not in the center, but at its edge, where it stabilized the overall feature." The brick was, in fact, found at the outermost edge of a stone circle, all that remained of a suspected conical pyramid that had collapsed. The brick would have indeed "stabilized" the steeply sloping sides of the sundial-like structure.

But the brick did more than provide support for the other stones heaped upon it. All of them, once they had been arranged into the completed pyramidal design, were infused by the Diviners or shamans with particular energy forms that produced a sense of emotional balance among the lake dwellers. This emotional harmony was a prerequisite for all further spiritual attainments and for the maintenance of social well-being. The single inverted ice-cream-cone-like pyramid could not generate sufficient energies alone, but did so in conjunction with several other, similar structures erected at strategic points around the former lake shore, their positions having been predetermined by the location of "power points" of natural energy in the earth.

The Bones

The knuckle bone was taken from a large, volcano-like stone mound, a family crypt, as it were, that contained the remains of many persons, as Lorraine envisioned. One of the deceased to whom the deer, a large buck, had been sacrificed was an old man who had outlived his family. Dying alone of some natural illness, he was honored as a visionary, whose prophecy about the end of the society that had gathered around Rock Lake could not prevent its inevitable collapse.

Marene keyed in on a very different person associated with the annular sepulcher. She saw a young girl, about thirteen years old, with long, dark hair, being escorted by her parents in some rite of passage, perhaps a coming-of-age ceremony. There was much joyful pageantry, including red and yellow flowers, nuts, berries, small squash, and the sacrificed deer, which followed in the procession laid out atop a tray with broad leafs, fronds resembling palms. The girl was surrounded by women bearing splendidly woven blankets draped over their arms in ritual fashion. The various colors of the blankets signified a different cardinal direction. Whether the maid celebrated this ceremony at the annular mound or was entombed in it, Marene was unable to determine. Our own scuba investigations suggested the monuments were indeed used for multiple purposes, not only for burials. They also served as astronomical observatories and focal points for ritual activities.

Although Linda correctly described the deer to which it long ago belonged, the smaller of the two bones elicited no particular response from her. Her reaction to the larger specimen was decidedly negative, however, because she immediately keyed into the animal's violent death, as part of the funeral feast that attended the entombment of an important person in one of the stone grave sites. But the stronger emotion sharpened her intuitive sense, and she not only properly identified the animal as a deer, but was able to determine that the bone came from its leg.

The Calcite Crystal

Lorraine felt the calcite had been brought up from beneath the earth by either flooding or ice, perhaps as long ago as twelve thousand years, when the glacier that carved out Rock Lake retreated to the north. Such finds at a place like Rock Lake are not accidental, Marene said, but part of the deliberately planned emergence of ancient greatness taking place as the planet's hour of ecological decision approaches. Persons involved in this re-emergence are assisted by angelic presences to bring certain meaningful elements together.

A cryptic statement she received while psychometrizing the calcite described the crystal as "an indication that all things are as they need to be." Linda's reading of the pyramidal calcite was likewise her most unproductive, perhaps because there really was not much to say about it. She knew, however, that it was once part of a modern rock collection. Judging from her responses and those of Lorraine and Marene, the crystal was not used by the prehistoric inhabitants, although all three women agreed that it could aid in meditation techniques, particularly where Rock Lake was concerned. The exact circumstances of the crystal's find were never established. All we were told was that it was discovered by a local resident either along the shore of Rock Lake or in shallow water in the 1920s. More than its pyramidal shape sparked our interest. Calcite crystal is not native to the Jefferson County area, so the specimen is an import. Also, calcite crystals have been found in the burials of shamans belonging to the Mississippian culture of the Upper Midwest. The Anker site, on the banks of the Little Calumet River, just south of Chicago, when excavated in 1960, was found to contain a calcite crystal similar to the Rock Lake example and associated with a shaman's grave.

The Pyramid Stone
The unremarkable looking little stone with traces of some questionable bonding material still clinging to its side prompted more detailed responses. It was taken from the Limnatis Pyramid, the Temple of the Moon itself, the linear stone mound more than a hundred feet long lying under sixty feet of water on what used to be the shoreline of Rock Lake, 3,500 years ago. Lorraine contemplated the gray stone as she turned it over in her hand, focusing on ancient images as her inner eye looked back to a time remote yet strangely familiar. She saw fires burning atop the colossal structure, symbols of the True Flame cult, whose followers knew how to conjure the dragon power or earth energies concentrated in the great monument specifically made for such purposes.

She saw young men chanting and singing as they built it. Their singing did more than pass the long hours of labor; it was an integral part of the enchantment that went into the ceremonial magic of the Temple of the Moon; to render the entire structure internally harmonious with all the forces of the cosmic order. They were joined by choruses of women who kept up a continual repertoire of songs, many of them intended to literally sing the sprits of the dead on their way to "the Realms of Perpetual Light." Remarkably, Marene envisioned identical choral singing for the same purposes.

When the workers finished its construction, they bowed reverentially toward the gleaming monument, then retreated to make way for the Diviners, the spiritual leaders and adepts, who inserted particularly chosen gems and minerals into special niches in the stonework. Some of these final additions included red-orange hixtonite and copper, the esoteric components that focused or otherwise directed planetary vibrations accumulating in the sacred mound like an invisible river of powerful, eternal energy. The enormous spiritual power thus available enabled them to perform what today would be considered miraculous feats of healing, clairvoyance, clairaudience, telepathy, levitation, inter-dimensional travel, and other paranormal achievements we can scarcely imagine.

Some of the inserted stones were included to be used when calling down the Angel of Death, a beneficent entity more like a spirit guide similar to the ancient Egyptian Anubis, an amiable being, who comforted and escorted the soul of someone recently deceased through the usual transition period of fear and disorientation from this life to the next.

Marene's inisghts were, of course, borne out by the excavations of the C.L. Lewis stone mound in Indiana and similar burial monuments throughout Ohio and Wisconsin, all of which contained mysterious ritual items made of copper. Her reading also suggests that the numerous instances of paranormal experiences chronicled at Rock Lake and Aztalan have been generated at least in part by the underwater structures, which, she said, were supercharged with so much intense spiritual energy. She reminds us, too, of the strange stone excavators found buried in its own chamber at Aztalan's Pyramid of the Moon. When presented to tribal elders from the Winnebago tribe, they shrank away in horror and without explanation from "the spirit stone."[4]

The Lost Poet

The remains of many persons were interred under the sunken Temple of the Moon, and it was on the lives of these people that Marene concentrated. She connected with two men, socially separated from each other but linked by a shared sense of despair they took with them into their common tomb. The younger of the two, while neither an aristocrat nor of royal blood, achieved some distinction in life as a craftsman and woodworker. But his profession left him unfulfilled, because his chief ambition was to be a writer. He considered himself "a lost poet." A traditional idealist who loved his civilization, he longed for a restoration of its former glory, which he saw ebbing away.

Marene feels he has since been reincarnated and is "back in the body" today. He died before he was forty years old.

The other man was middle aged when he passed away and likewise unhappy with the cultural decline of the society he helped to found. In fact, it might not be far from the truth to say he died of despair, having lost the will to live in a world degenerating beyond his control.

His death is somehow associated with a large, metal blade resembling a modern farm implement, suggesting, perhaps incorrectly, suicide. The man was very tall, of medium complexion, physically powerful and in possession of a suspicious, very alert intellect—a leader, who arrived in Wisconsin on a civilizing mission from very far away (Atlantis?). But his hopes were only partially realized: "He longed for some place he could get back to or for some peak experience he was unable to repeat. Out of this sense of loss, realization eventually overwhelmed his hopes. Things would not change for the better after all, and wistfulness for the lost golden age dissipated over the years into despair."

The large blade Marene saw entombed in the underwater mound finds its correspondent in a virtually identical structure on dry land, the C.L. Lewis stone mound just cited above. There, too, an oversized dagger was associated with the skeleton of a tall man, whose prominent social standing was confirmed by his gorget and other badges of authority. The Indiana knife was made of chalcedony and Marene saw the Rock Lake blade as metal, but they both appear to have been among the regalia of high-ranking officials belonging to the same culture. Parallel physical evidence of this kind tends to confirm the accuracy of Marene's psychic vision, while providing us with unprecedented insight into the very core of the sunken monument and deeper still into the past lives of its honored dead.

A happier echo Marene picked up belonged to a young woman of childlike beauty and goodness ("innocence and awareness combined"), surprisingly blond, which enhanced her angelic appearance. Among the very earliest inhabitants of Rock Lake, then known as Tirajana, she belonged to the High Order, an advanced level of divination within the cult of the True Flame.

In life, she possessed a naturally serene and composed character, owing perhaps to her personal conduct, as was required within the precepts of cosmic harmony. But she was also emotionally thrilled about something in her life, perhaps a lover, but her own devotion to and enthusiasm for the High Order was such, she might have died while in some spiritual fervor. Despite her death in the prime of youthful bloom, her funeral was a joyous celebration filled with "beautiful vibrations," because her surviving co-religionists believed she had been especially honored by the gods, who, envying human perfection and as a sign of their favor, took her directly into their blessed realms. Her services comprised a great deal of happy music, mostly community singing and chanting accompanied by choirs of high-pitched flutes, all intended to send her off on her joyful transition.

Who Lies Within the Tomb?
Lorraine's vision of Rock Lake's underwater necropolis complemented Marene's characterization of the long, tentlike stone mound as a tomb for honored non-royalty, while the high rulers reposed under their own conical structures:

"Yes, there are several, usually placed in their own cone. The scientists, priests, shamans and occasional sky-being used the smaller individual cone. After the spirit left the physical body, the remains were placed in a cone. Cones were used over and over. The long 'tepee' held the workers, their managers, and the transporter crews who harvested the copper. These rock tepees were open to receive corpses. It was found that they could be rapidly transformed by positioning them at the joining point of the energy lines below the lake."

Linda's favorite member of the Rock Lake collection was its most physically unimpressive. Looking at this unprepossessing rock, nothing about its ordinary appearance suggests the dramatic circumstances of its origins in the sunken Temple of the Moon. Yet she used its inherent vibrations to accurately describe the drowned monument and beyond it to the vanished world it once dominated:

"This little stone comes from a very large formation that, seen from above, resembles a three-story building lying on its side. It was oriented on a north-south line and stood at the edge of the shore, overlooking the lake. The structure, once coated with some kind of whitish substance, is very old.

"This stone, like the thousands of others it was once a part of, weighed down on top of ashes, the ashes of human bones. There was a great deal of fire associated with this building, inside it; not a fire of destruction, but a life-giving fire. There is a life-death theme surrounding this place. A lot of chanting was going on while it was being built. The monument is 'enchanted,' spiritually charged. I feel heavy rain, a lot of water on it. The waters rose high over it. Now there is silt all around the base."

Linda's reading is an amazing recreation of the Limnatis Pyramid, the Temple of the Moon, which is graphically described, for any of the divers who have seen it, as "a three-story building lying on its side." So too, it was oriented on a north-south axis, stood on Rock Lake's former shoreline thirty-five centuries ago, was coated with a white lime plaster and, if identical stone mounds throughout the Midwest are anything to go by, contains the buried remains of the prehistoric inhabitants. Here the cult of the True Flame is again in evidence, as is her parallel reading with Marene of the singing that accompanied the monument's construction.

All three psychics gave reports that were remarkably complimentary. Their readings may be likened to the observations of three persons looking at an object from different positions; they all see the same thing, but from individual points of view. Their combined testimony has more than a ring of truth; much of it may be verified by hard material evidence. It was their extraordinary vision, however, which saw beyond the physical limitations of our five senses and presented us with a view of the past otherwise denied mortals.

•13•

The Return of the
Beaded Princess

*The entity then was a Princess in the Temple of the Sun, or
the Temple of Light. There the entity made overtures not only
to its own people, but to those of many lands.*

—*Edgar Cayce*

M arene Martensen has done so much good work with the
powerful feminine energies at Aztalan's Pyramid of the
Moon, that I was particularly interested to learn about her
psychic impressions of the so-called "Beaded Princess"—that mysterious lady laid in an opulent funeral garb under her own mound outside the enclosure's high walls. Happily, Marene quickly picked up on
the lingering vibrations of the Princess and shared with me a reading
especially memorable for its credibility and humanity.

As she spoke, I thought back to my own, more mundane research
into one of the most intriguing finds ever made by American archaeologists. In 1911, they began to excavate a rather unprepossessing
mound a few hundred feet north of Aztalan's stockaded walls. The
squat, conical earthwork today stands about four feet high, with a
base of some fifteen feet. In its prehistoric condition, it was two feet
taller and twice its present diameter, but erosional forces over the
past eight centuries have reduced its original dimensions.

Expecting to find little or nothing of real importance, the investigators were astounded to uncover the most luxuriant pre-Columbian

burial north of the Rio Grande. Its antiquity could not be doubted. The grave site dated back to the first days of Aztalan's Late Mississippian phase, circa A.D. 1100, when the ceremonial center suddenly experienced a dramatic upsurge in population and the outstanding features of its material accomplishments took place.

The eight-hundred-year-old tomb contained the well-preserved skeleton of a woman five feet, seven inches tall. She died of natural causes (which may have had something to do with her spinal deformity) around her twenty-eighth birthday. Her corpse had been wrapped in a full-length envelope of bark.

But it was her funeral garb that elicited the greatest astonishment from her modern discoverers. It comprised three fabulous belts of polished mother-of-pearl beads expertly crafted into circles, squares, and triangles. Her necklace alone contained 585 beads; another 846 went into her belt, and 547 made up a pattern that went around the hem of her dress. Altogether, she wore no less than 1,978 individually hand-cut beads. There was some equivocal evidence for a crown or headgear of some kind, possibly a thin headband of beaten copper with feathers, but this element had decayed too far for positive identification.

Less uncertain were the lady's earrings, which were perfectly preserved. They were very small, each less than an inch in diameter, superbly fashioned from high-grade copper and made to represent a pair of male human heads. As we shall see, both Marene and Lorraine felt the Beaded Princess originated among the great pre-Columbian civilizations of Middle America. Material evidence connecting Wisconsin with ancient Peru exists in a golden necklace of stylized human heads from a tomb in Sipán. Although this find belongs to the Moche civilization, which predates the Aztalan, it represents an ornamental motif associated with an area comprising northern Peru to Yucatan and worn by the Beaded Princess.

The image evokes recollections of Red Horn, the strangely fair-haired hero of Winnebago myth whom Dr. Robert Salzer believes is associated with the fate of ancient Aztalan. We are reminded, too, of the twin inverted skulls placed nearly a thousand years ago at the precise center point of Aztalan, whence they faced exactly east and west.

Then there is the Headless Man Mound only a few miles from Aztalan itself, and the nearby burial of a real man who appears to have been ritually decapitated. And let us not forget the stone mound of a headless man five fathoms deep in the northeast quadrant of Rock Lake. Obviously, a powerful and important theme once ran from the lake to the ceremonial city and its entombed "Beaded Princess."

That was the name she soon acquired after her removal from her burial mound at Aztalan to the Milwaukee Public Museum, forty miles to the east. Her remains were put in a glassed-in display that attracted attention from around the country. But some months after popular interest wore off, her bones and splendid beadwork were unceremoniously cataloged and shelved in a drawer in the museum basement, where they lie to this day.

Residents of Jefferson County, particularly those in the modern town of Aztalan, have repeatedly called for her return, and there is some lingering resentment of Milwaukee officials who continue to ignore all such appeals. That she may indeed have been a "princess" is entirely possible, although most researchers generally believe she was something more, probably a shaman, a spiritually gifted woman, who served as a physical and emotional healer and as an ambassador of heaven on Earth. The richness of her burial gown attests to the particularly high regard in which she was held by her civilization. Had she ever worn such raiment in real life, her appearance would have been nothing short of spectacular but nevertheless in keeping with her status as the supreme religious figure of ancient Aztalan in the days of its glory.

I was aware of the archaeological and mythic implications of the Beaded Princess as Marene Martensen began to connect with something else I could not intellectually define, but somehow sensed.

The Name of the Princess
Aztalan was established with a great deal of joy, expectation, and enthusiasm, she said. But shortly thereafter, the newcomers were beset by many problems which adversely affected their morale. It was at this critical time that Katalani appeared. (Katalani was the real name of the Beaded Princess). She was born in Yucatan and brought specifically to Aztalan for healing purposes, but her greatness went beyond merely physical assistance and revitalized a whole community at a critical moment in its development. She and her father came with the "Ship People," or Sea People, mariners in charge of transporting entire groups of "Land People" to their destination and helping them organize the area chosen for resettlement. The Ship People were the trading merchants who always traveled far, bringing news as well as commerce and serving as roving cultural ambassadors.

Katalani preferred the freer, more adventurous life of the Ship People to the sedentary existence of the Land People, to which she had been assigned. She smothered her longing for her former life in Yucatan, with its promise of distant travels, under a sense of duty to the Aztalaners. They desperately needed her inspiration and knew the ceremonial city would fail if she ever left.

She was not royalty but belonged to a lower aristocracy. Everyone was in awe of her, due to her spinal deformity, although she was allowed to grow up as a normal child. Things began to change in her life after she reached her twelfth year, when she rapidly began to develop her acute psychic powers. She was definitely gifted, and the priests took her under their care for a time, although she never became a shaman in the usual sense. Katalani was more of a seer and an emotional healer. She became enormously popular.

She was famous beyond the forbidding walls of her new home and wildly, almost desperately, adored as a national treasure because of her perfect spiritual love, the basis for all her paranormal abilities. It flowed always out of her innocence and inexhaustible kindness. There really was no one else like her. The people valued her as a gift from God, as someone sent by celestial beings to ease their burden during hard times. They saw her as a living sign from heaven not to despair, so she played a very important role in the early years of Aztalan, shortly after the beginning of the twelfth century A.D.

Despite her deformity, Katalani was not unattractive. Particularly outstanding were her slender hands with their very long fingers. Her face was dominated by her eyes. They were deep-set, unusually expressive, with an unfathomable, inward, and pensive quality her people found strange, almost frightening. Unlike their eyes, hers were hazel, because she was of mixed descent, the second generation offspring of a native Amerindian mother and the father who brought her from far away. Katalani had high cheekbones, and her forehead was higher and more prominent than that of other women. Even as an adult, she possessed a childlike smile among a generally unsmiling populace. Her long, dark, auburn hair was often ornamented with inch-long pins, like narrow tablets of bone, and little oblong beads made of shell.

Her Appearance in Aztalan

Beginning in her early years, she was taken to Aztalan's Pyramid of the Moon for healing and to keep up her health, in spite of her deformity. In winter, the people around her wore two-layered tunics and fur hats. During her lifetime, there was much music at Aztalan. Some of the instruments used then were 1½-inch-long finger cymbals shaped into triangles or concave circles and long sticks fastened with flat strips of metal. Each sound vibrated at a specific frequency to generate particular spiritual energies. The copper harmonized masculine, the shells feminine energies. But these instruments mostly accompanied community singing.

As she grew older, Katalani became more adept at the spiritual arts and was doing some esoteric work on a more universal level. She was always besieged by visitors, not only for her psychic readings, but just so people could be spiritually nourished by her blessed aura. They presented her with many gifts. These usually consisted of food, feathers (for both ornamental and religious purposes), and beautifully woven textiles, mostly mats. She also received mother-of-pearl, precious stones, and sometimes calcite pieces wrapped in animal hides. (We recall the calcite crystal found at Rock Lake and examined by Marene and her colleagues.)

Katalani did not marry, because she was considered too sacred for childbearing. She was always cheerful, but, due to her invaluable position in the community, she never left the enclosure after her arrival. Sometimes she yearned to know more about the world beyond the obscuring walls of Aztalan. She missed the traveling life of the Ship People she had known only too briefly earlier in life with her father, and she consequently suffered occasional bouts of melancholy.

When only twenty-six or twenty-seven years old and at the height of her popular adoration, she entered into a long illness. It began as congestion in the chest cavity, then developed into pneumonia or tuberculosis. A large boat carrying medical specialists from far away docked at Aztalan on the Crawfish River. They tried to effect a lasting cure, but her condition had advanced ahead of their skill to save her.

Mourning for her death spread far beyond the ceremonial city, but her people understood that Katalani had been sent directly to them in their time of crisis, since passed, and that she had only returned to the blessed regions from which she came. Her fabulous burial garment was never worn while she lived, but it had been prepared for her transformation long in advance.

Her funeral was very ritualistic. Only fifty to a hundred persons were allowed to attend, and even these participants were divided into two circles. Both were open to the north from the eastern to the western horizons. The two distinct circles represented two separate ceremonies, and things needed to be done in a certain, prescribed fashion. There was much singing, no lamenting, in the hope that positive harmonies would help speed her soul on its way. The funeral orientation was definitely toward the north, the spirit direction. She died around A.D. 1130, although her memory was venerated by subsequent generations of Aztalaners until the collapse of their society, some two hundred years later. Flowers were regularly placed on her burial mound during special ceremonies involving groups of small children.

Through meditation, prayer, or ritual, we may still access something of Katalani's spirit essence at the Pyramid of the Moon.

"I don't mean to say we can expect to enter into a regular dialogue with her," Marene explained. "Instead, we can experience her enduring benevolence and the well-being of wholeness she generated in life."

Lorraine's reading was strikingly similar in many details, although she described at greater length some aspects only touched on by Marene. She agreed that the Beaded Princess was the child of a native American woman and an alien father. His name was Zaetock Mezantl. He was an important personage from Mexico, who belonged to an elite group of culture-bearers, keepers of high wisdom, and wielders of political influence. Their task was not only to preserve scientific and spiritual knowledge, but to act as the founders of new cities and ceremonial centers throughout the Americas. Lorraine's characterization of these roving founding fathers parallels Marene's description of the Ship People who brought Katalani to Aztalan.

Zaetock Mezantl was among the culture-bearers who arrived in southern Wisconsin from coastal Yucatan at a place called Tulum. Lorraine's insight was extraordinary in this instance, because one of the earliest archaeologists to excavate Aztalan in the 1930s for the Milwaukee Public Museum theorized that the Aztalaners originated at Tulum, in view of the close resemblance between the Wisconsin and Yucatan sites.[1]

Tulum

A closer look at Tulum reveals that, like Aztalan, it was surrounded by a rectangular wall with watchtowers and was completely covered by a white limestone plaster, atypical building techniques for the Mayas, who built no other walled ceremonial centers. The Mexican enclosure featured a plaza, ritual area, trapezoidal pyramids, and a secluded residential section, the same elements recurring at the Wisconsin city. Both sites were open to water on the east and both were commercial centers at the hub of vast trading networks connected by river and

El Castillo at Tulum

coastal routes. They even shared an important cultural common denominator in astronomy: "The time of the summer and winter solstices and the vernal and autumnal equinoxes [at Tulum] determined the work patterns and religious events."[2]

Aztalan was outstanding for its solar, lunar, and stellar alignments, particularly those marking the solstices. It seems clear, then, that it received direct influence from Yucatan as its primary founding impetus; that culture-bearers, among them Katalani's father, made the long voyage from coastal Mexico to establish a similar site in southern Wisconsin. This conclusion is underscored by the foundation of Aztalan in A.D. 1100 and the abandonment of Tulum just previous to that date in post-Classic times.

Intrigued by the apparent parallels between Tulum and Aztalan, I traveled to the ancient ceremonial center on the Yucatan coast in early January 1995. Nine years earlier, I had visited this archaeologically rich region of Mexico but had bypassed the "City of the Dawn," failing then to discern any conceivable links with distant Wisconsin. But now, as I walked though the main entrance from the west, I was immediately impressed by the site's resemblance to the pyramid complex on the banks of the far-off Crawfish River.

Tulum is certainly one of the most beautiful and evocative places in the world. Hemmed in on the west by the lush green of a vast jungle forest infested with alligators and on the east by the pristine beaches and turquoise waters of the Caribbean, its white limestone temples are set within a thirty-six-square-acre precinct surrounded on three sides by a wall three-quarters of a mile long. The city perches at the edge of a forty-foot high cliff overlooking the sea, while red tropical flowers make a naturally romantic contrast against the bleached ruins under a never-failing sun.

Visitors do not need to know anything of Tulum's past to appreciate its physical loveliness. But to examine that past is to deepen one's appreciation of the place. At the zenith of its power, around A.D. 1000, Tulum was a brilliant complex of structures adorned with murals painted crimson, pastel white, indigo, and black. Only faint traces of those colors and a single set of murals still survive. Among the most interesting are the red prints of hands impressed on the interior walls of El Castillo, the so-called "Citadel," the site's largest building.

It and the other temples were finished during post-Classic times, in the twelfth century, but they were built upon lower cultural plateaus going back through previous, earlier stages to deeply prehistoric times. The structures visitors see today are but the last stylistic developments of Mayan (or maybe even pre-Mayan) development over the course of perhaps millennia of construction, one level upon the next. It is this mix of deeply ancient origins and very late development at Tulum that links the site simultaneously backward and forward in time—a possible link between Atlantis and Wisconsin.

The city's earliest known name was Zama, from Itzamna, a culture hero the Mayas remembered as their founding father. They portrayed him in temple art as a bearded figure, who arrived in Yucatan with all the technology and high wisdom of some outside civilization. He was accompanied by his wife, Ixchel, literally, "the White Lady," and both were survivors from a great flood that destroyed their distant homeland over the sea.

Zama also appears in "Zonzama," the Bronze Age citadel on the Canary Island of Lanzarote, off the North African shores of Morocco. Readers of *The Lost Pyramids of Rock Lake* will recall that the stone monuments under the waters of Rock Lake were traced back to civilizers (specifically copper entrepreneurs) from the Canaries, 3,500 years ago. Those islands were in the immediate sphere of Atlantean influence, a connection with Tulum underscored by the obvious Atlantean identities of Itzamna and Ixchel. Moreover, the sacred numeral of Atlantis, five, and the red-white-black construction colors described by Plato occur in the very architecture of Tulum, just as they did in the sunken capital; i.e., the five ritual entrances in the walls and the early Mayas' preference for painting murals with red, white, and black pigments.

The Descending God
Among the most perplexing and perhaps Atlantean features of Tulum is the figure of the so-called "Descending God." No one knows the real identity or function of this personage depicted in stone relief on various temples in Tulum. He is portrayed as a young man diving into the water. He may represent Itzamna or some other survivor diving into the water from sinking Atlantis.

The Descending God may personify early culture-bearers who escaped the Great Flood and brought civilization to Yucatan, as described in Mayan legend. Tulum was, after all, dedicated to Itzamna, Ixchel, and Chac, the rain god, whose resemblance to Atlas, the eponymous figure of Atlantis, is unmistakable. Like Atlas, Chac was envisioned as a man bearing the sky on his shoulders and was the patron of astrology-astronomy (there being made no distinction between the two sciences in either the Old or New Worlds). It seems probable that Tulum (or Zama, its earlier name) was among the first cities built by the Atlanteans in Middle America, a heritage memorialized in its Descending God. Plato, in fact, tells us that Atlantis had a colony called Azaes, which bears a philological resemblance to the Itzas, the followers of Itzamna.

The Descending God has been identified by R. Gordon Wasson as the Aztec Teopiltzintli, or Piltzintli, revered to this day throughout the Valley of Mexico in his Christian guise as Santo Niño de Atocha. He could be a significant link between Tulum and Aztalan, because Teopiltzintli was the god of mass migrations, the spiritual leader of a whole people or nation from one location to another.

It was the Diving God who, the Aztecs believed, led their forefathers from an ancestral homeland, Aztlan, a great island in the Sunrise Sea, the Atlantic Ocean, before it was destroyed by a cataclysmic deluge.[3] His stylized portrayal shows him diving into the water to escape the destruction of Aztlan. Teopiltzintli's oceanic origin is emphasized by the gifts with which his worshippers revere him—seashells—and the paved ceremonial road leading from his temple at Tulum directly to the shore.

Indeed, the orientation of Tulum and its smaller shrine due north on the coast is entirely toward the sea. As the ancestral leader of mass migrations, his prominence there is appropriate to the wholesale relocation of a population from Yucatan to Wisconsin. Needless to add, the myth is an obvious echo of Mesoamerica's seminal ancestral event; namely, migrations of survivors to Yucatan from the destruction of Atlantis (Aztlan).

If, like the fading colors of the original paint, we may also discern faint traces of Atlantis at Tulum, telltale evidence for Aztlan, so much nearer to us in time, is more obvious. As the post-Classic building styles were superimposed on previous cultural strata, so the themes that connect Tulum with Wisconsin lay upon the earlier Atlantean motifs.

First, there is the wall, from which the city took its name. It is the only one of its kind in all Mesoamerica. Twenty feet high and wider by a foot at its base, it was interspersed with square watchtowers and bonded with a limestone cement. The wall formed a rectangle guarding north, west, and south, with the city open to the east and the sea. This is the same otherwise unique arrangement found at Aztalan, where the outer wall, plastered over in limestone cement, was open to the east on the Crawfish River.

Tulum's wall possessed another singular feature duplicated only in Aztalan; namely, an interior walkway that connected one watchtower with another. A bright fire beacon blazed from the top of El Castillo, while Aztalan featured similar beacons from great cauldrons fixed to the top of its exterior wall. It was this wall that separated an aristocracy of shamans, military leaders, astronomers, priests, captains, and labor organizers from the toiling masses of hunters, farmers, sailors, and artisans who dwelt outside the Wisconsin enclosure. The same class distinction was effected by a similar wall at Tulum.

A Wisconsin Connection
Both sites were trading centers, where imported goods from the Gulf of Mexico were collected and bartered for local goods. The bodies incinerated at Aztalan's crematorium in the Pyramid of the Moon were oriented to the rising of Venus, just as Tulum's Temple of the Descending God was dedicated to the same planet. The number three, which played such an important role in the construction of Aztalan,

Northwest watchtower at Tulum

is likewise found at Tulum, with its three terraced stories. These comparisons go beyond coincidental parallels and assume credible importance when we learn that Tulum was suddenly abandoned at the same time Aztalan began, just as abruptly, around A.D. 1100. Although the Yucatan city continued to be occupied by various groups until 1500, its early post-Classic aristocracy appears to have deserted Tulum in the twelfth century.

Does all this mean that the Mayan leadership of Tulum left Yucatan around A.D. 1100 by sailing the eastern coast into the Gulf of Mexico, up the Mississippi River and its tributaries to Wisconsin, where they built Aztalan? Archaeologists do not credit the Mayas as being very great sailors. Yet Tulum was unquestionably a sea-oriented city, with its fire beacon, visible for many miles out on the ocean, and its natural docking area. Its Descending God diving into the water certainly implies a people involved in maritime activities. In examining the numerous and important points of reference between Tulum and Aztalan, one cannot deny the suspicion that here, at least, psychic impressions tend to be validated by material evidence found in the archaeological record.

Tulum has at least one other unusual feature which may have some bearing on its identity as a shamanistic center. Precisely four hundred meters due east from the cove sheltering under the cliff that supports El Castillo is a large "blue hole." Among the unexplained mysteries of the sea, blue holes are perfectly circular areas varying in diameter from a few feet to several yards and extraordinary for their brilliant blue color. They appear in shallow depths, sometimes in only a foot or so of water, but are like vertical tunnels going straight down unknown fathoms.

Oceanographers do not understand how they are formed, nor to what depths they sink, while some speculate the phenomenon is related to the sudden disappearances of ships in the Bermuda Triangle. In any case, the existence of a blue hole just out from Tulum may have had some bearing on the Mayan geomancers' choice of this particular Yucatan cliff for the location of their ceremonial center.

But origins from Tulum do not obviate Aztalan's early relationship with Cahokia, some of whose inhabitants abandoned their Mississippian megalopolis in south-central Illinois at the same moment Aztalan was founded. They migrated northward, because their ceremonial calendar told them the time had come for them to leave.[4] This was the same sacred calendar in use throughout Mesoamerica, including Tulum, where the priests, reading shared celestial information and reaching identical astronomical conclusions, joined the ritual trek to the north.

Katalini's father, Zaetek Mazantl, was among those founders of Aztalan from Tulum, and Lorraine Darr's psychic view of this deep past is in agreement with the archaeological record. He was tall, she said, and slender, of reddish auburn hair, because, as an aristocrat, he carried the blood of the ancient Sea Peoples in his veins. He wore a golden gorget suspended by a chain around his neck and silver bracelets on his forearms. These ornaments were badges of office and authority. The gorget, about six inches in diameter, was fashioned to resemble the sun on one side, the rays streaming outward from the disc; its obverse bore occult symbols or hieroglyphics.

Katalani herself was committed to worshipping the sun god and moon goddess and played central roles in religious pageantry honoring the chief deities of Aztalan at their two temple mounds. The other performers in these spiritual dramas dressed elaborately to impersonate the seasons, the wind, the weather, and particularly animals, such as dogs, birds, and deer—all of which were regarded as divine entities. Katalani was a visionary who could communicate with these gods and was beloved by her people as "a star encased in human form."

Dream-Maker
While Lorraine's reading of the Beaded Princess complemented
Marene's impressions and went beyond them to Yucatan origins,
Linda focused in greater detail on Katalani's physical appearance:
"She liked to wear a tall, white plume, almost like an ostrich
feather, in her long, straight hair. She was given many rings, but her
two favorites included a small turquoise on a golden band and a black
onyx set into gold almost like a mosaic. She sometimes wore a head-
dress composed of beads hanging in strings, which were marks of
social and priestly rank. More often, she wore a simple headband
around her forehead as a device of some kind to aid her developing
Third Eye, the pineal gland associated with psychic vision. [In fact,
archaeologists found the remains of a copper headband around the
skull of the Beaded Princess.]

"She bore only a partial facial resemblance to the Indian residents
of southern Wisconsin. Her cast of features, such as her distinctive
Mayan nose, suggested Mesoamerican origins. She had artificially dis-
tended ear lobes, an upper class style of the time much favored by
Middle American aristocrats, in which were hung yellow and blue
gems or looping copper earrings. Less for ornament than for the spiritual protection it provided, a copper cross signifying the four cardinal
directions was worn on her left forearm.

"Katalani often appeared in state sitting atop Aztalan's Pyramid of
the Moon in a chair especially made to accommodate her deformity.
She had to be helped into it by the two guards who stood on either
side of her. They each held a red staff with three yellow plumes rising
from the top. The men wore loincloths about their waists, copper gor-
gets around their necks, and golden armbands. From her throne on
the temple mound, she played the role of counselor and seer. It was
also her mission to explain the lessons of the old culture to the new
one and to pull the whole community together in its time of crisis. The
people hailed her as the Princess of Vision, the Lady Who Waits,
Dream-maker, Prophetess, and the Princess of the Night.

"While she enjoyed these honors, her real happiness was a flower
garden adjacent to her house. In it she grew yellow, blue, pink, and
mauve blossoms, some of which she used for herbal brews to induce
visions. She frequently collected little bouquets and placed them
around her doorstep to attract children, which always delighted her.
She was also a great animal lover, especially of small creatures like
fauns and birds. Her favorite was a wild crow with a single white

feather under one of its wings. Its appearance in her vicinity was always regarded as portentous and helped her predict future events, which she interpreted in the bird's movements. It was during one such visit in our month of January that she was able to foretell her own death.

"She asked that the spring equinox ceremony, which she loved dearly, be held one month early, an unheard of request only someone of her supreme spiritual stature could make. The priests, although dismayed at the change, accommodated her and she once more, for the last time, saw the great religious drama that heralded the return of life in the spring. Now she could die contented, she said, and promised to give two signs in the natural world that would tell her people that her soul had survived death. One year to the day after her funeral, the sun would rise orange in the morning with a yellow halo around it, and just as the sun stood above the horizon, a crane-like bird never seen in Aztalan before would fly across the dawn. When this solar phenomenon came to pass, as it did, the Aztalaners felt their bond with Katalani had been renewed. The other prophecy was likewise a new covenant with her people, when certain herbal flowers began to grow of their own accord on her burial mound. As they did when she left bouquets near her home, the new blossoms attracted generations of children who frolicked around her grave site."

•14•

A Psychic Overview
of Rock Lake and Aztalan

*The entity was among those Atlanteans who remained. Thus
again the interest in things psychic, things mysterious, things
unseen.*

—*Edgar Cayce*

Independently of each other, Lorraine, Marene, and Linda used the
term "gateway" to describe Rock Lake. They meant that its waters
cover and comprise one of the planet's great cross-points and con-
centrations of earth energy. Such places have been considered sacred
sites for thousands of years, because they have an innate power to
alter human consciousness and open it to the Otherworld of dimensions beyond our day-to-day physical existence.

It was this high spiritual quality that attracted the location's earliest visitors unknown centuries ago and continues to fascinate modern investigators. Through such a gateway many things may be
accessed, including interdimensional time travel, which is responsible
for the fleeting appearance and inexplicable disappearance of the surface rocks and subsurface buildings observed by lake residents and
scuba divers, respectively. If these energies continue to operate hap-
hazardly, it means they still function but are no longer directed, the
means for their proper use having been lost with the fall of civilization
in prehistoric Wisconsin 700 years ago.

While some of the underwater monuments may be hiding under the silt, others vanish, not behind a curtain of algae bloom, but into another dimension beyond our time. As a portal between life and death, the place teems with spirits from numerous levels of existence, according to Lorraine, who sees them in the thick mists often covering the waters. It is the same misty spirit energy envisioned by Linda, who has never visited the lake.

Many of these entities are the souls of men and women who flourished around Rock Lake in the deep past. Still others have since reincarnated in some of the present townspeople and especially among the investigators who are powerfully and otherwise so mysteriously drawn to the lake. It also acts as a 1,371-square-acre psychic capacitor for telepathy, scrying, past life regression, and virtually every other paranormal activity.

"It is a broadcast place," says Lorraine.

But she claims it is also protected by a spirit guardian conjured there in the form of a terrible serpent by the high magic (the lost psychic technology) of the Diviners to preserve their necropolis from harm. An Oneida Indian who attended our first sonar exploration of the lake in 1989 and another tribal member we met three years later identically described a large serpentine creature dwelling in the lake. Lorraine says it lies in any number of holes at the bottom, like a gargantuan eel. They were first spotted in the mid-1930s by free divers, who described them as "Indian shafts."[1]

Being a kind of programmed monster, he cannot cause anyone physical harm in the same way a shark is able to do. But he is powerful enough to alter his material environment, such as covering the monuments in veils of silt, dispatching them into another dimension, or subtly altering the consciousness of a diver so that he may look directly at them without seeing them or spoiling attempts at photography by sabotaging his film or equipment.

At the Guardian's Discretion
The degree of a diver's success in finding one of the pyramids depends on the level of his own spiritual development. As Lorraine said, "the guardian scrutinizes the heart of anyone who enters its domain. It can perceive the light of an individual's soul, upon which it determines a course of action, a response to the intruder."

The guardian's strength proportionately increases with the light level generated by the soul of a diver. Theoretically, the creature is powerless if confronted by a highly enlightened and spiritually evolved person, who would be sensitive to all the lake's secrets. Some investigators argue such a visitor would only attempt to find the sunken monuments for the most pressing spiritual reasons, or more likely never venture into the lake out of respect for its honored dead.

Less enlightened visitors still experience intensifying strata of fear the deeper they descend into its frigid, darkening depths. One can certainly feel an aura of death or the growing anger of some coiled menace lurking unseen in the cold, black waters. While the spirit guardian has so far refrained from severely harming anyone, so far as is known, it could conceivably injure or kill if, for example, it suddenly revealed itself to a diver, who, in a panic, rose too quickly to the surface and contracted air embolism, better known as "the bends." To help minimize the potential for such trauma, Marene advises making an offering of sage or tobacco, long regarded as sacred herbs, on the face of the waters, together with a brief prayer expressing one's good intentions. Crystals or other special stones also make assuaging gifts.

Perhaps most of the coldly rational professionals who seem unable to find Rock Lake's sunken structures have been prevented from seeing them by the spirit guardian because they suppress their spiritual nature. As for the prehistoric people of Rock Lake and Aztalan, they belonged to many physical types.

"America has been a melting pot many thousands of years before the Statue of Liberty was set up at Staten Island," Lorraine said. The old blood from Atlantis and its allied islands, the Canaries, flowed through here, as did that of Central American culture bearers many centuries later. There were the Plains Indians or tribal wanderers, certainly the very earliest visitors to Wisconsin, at least as long as twelve thousand years ago. The world around them was alive with the soul of Nature, which they perceived and venerated everywhere. It was for them that which Yeats exclaimed in poetry: "Everything we look upon is blest!"

Linda felt that the abundant energies she and her colleagues interpreted at Rock Lake and Aztalan were not, after all, supernatural phenomena, but nothing more than the fundamental laws of cause and effect. They only seem incredible or miraculous to us now, because we have forgotten how to use them. That psychic heritage from our ancestors, who were familiar with the application of spiritual forces to influence material reality, almost completely vanished when their civilization died out. That is why investigating and recreating their past is so important; namely, to find the lost treasures of our paranormal heritage for use in our overly materialist world.

Spiritual Energies Tapped for Material Power

The territory the Aztalaners and their Atlantean predecessors controlled was not only so much real estate in the Midwest, but multidimensional on several levels of being, physical and psychical. The mighty energy lines which criss-crossed under Rock Lake/Aztalan made it possible for the original inhabitants to achieve many of their paranormal endeavors.

Linda believes these lines extended beyond their own physical dimensions of space and time: "The Diviners were busy with healing, astral projection, telepathy, clairvoyance, clairaudience, the application of telluric power for the construction of great building projects, prospecting for precious metals, manipulation of the native peoples for political and economic purposes, alteration of the natural environment, even communication with spiritual entities which today might be called 'extraterrestrial' intelligences.

"There were too many experiments for power," she said.

"Ambition for omnipotence got out of hand, but such zeal typified the times, of which the lake dwellers were only a part.

"In those days, Rock Lake was an outpost, whose relationship to Atlantis was the same as Texas is today to the U.S., because the Wisconsin stone monuments were made in the epoch when the Atlantean imperium dominated much of the northern hemisphere. Its empire was so far-flung, researchers who have claimed that Atlantis was in this location or that, fail to understand that the civilization it developed took root in many parts of the world. Many Atlanteans went to Rock Lake over the years and they installed one of their "power crystals," which facilitated telepathy with the motherland on an island in the Atlantic Ocean."

Adepts trained in the use of the crystal were able to open lines of mental communication with other outposts throughout the empire, particularly in Florida and Bimini, in the Bahamas, where Linda envisioned a great many ruins from those times under the waters of the Caribbean.

"The early civilizers at Rock Lake arrived from the direction of their home island, in the east. They were wide-ranging travelers before and after they arrived to set up trading networks from the Upper Great Lakes Region to South America."

Unaware of the ancients' copper mining enterprise at the Michi-gan-Canadian border, or of their commercial ties to Ecuador and Peru, Linda's description of prehistoric Wisconsin's connection to Andean America is right on the money.

"They were an advanced people much involved in politics and trade, but the spiritual side of life mattered most to them. Their holy city presently under water once spread beyond the present shoreline. And I see a metallic triangle or pyramid-shaped object, which was somehow related to the source of their esoteric power, or its leading symbol."

Interestingly, a large delta platform lies under the south end of Rock Lake, and a curious metallic (copper) triangular pendant was, in fact, discovered during the first archaeological excavation of Aztalan.

"But a pole shift occurred that caused numerous worldwide cata-strophes, including the destruction of Atlantis. The Diviners saw it coming and they tried to re-establish the world's geological equilib-rium. That is the main reason for all those conical pyramids. Every-thing got chaotic, the city was inundated, and most of the residents fled. A handful of individuals were ordered to remain behind for some reason, and rescue parties were later sent back to save them from hostile natives. Survival was the only thing anybody cared about then, but they took the great crystal, which was really not very large, with them from the center of the city before it went under. Disasters forced everyone out. Before the last of them left, the Diviners conjured spirit guardians into the lake to protect the sunken shrines and graves for-ever. They are still there.

"But the sacred site was never forgotten. Outsiders were drawn to it over the centuries for spiritual replenishment, although they always moved on. There are echoes of several different languages around the lakeshore, not all of them local Indian or modern Euro-pean. The area experienced a second era of civilized greatness, but it did not last as long as its first period (the Atlantean epoch)."

Linda here refers to the two-hundred-year existence of Aztalan, after A.D. 1100, of which she knew absolutely nothing, consciously.

"Afterwards, everything was almost entirely forgotten until the last century, when people began taking interest in the site again.

"There are many more monuments in the lake than have thus far been accounted for, but most of them are covered over by great quan-tities of mud and silt, so finding them is not likely."

Linda's concluding reflection added a personal concern: "Some-how, I feel all of us who have been engaged in this project are related to one another through the first people who resided at Rock Lake and Aztalan in the deep past. Yes, we are certainly related to them in a way I strongly feel but cannot adequately explain. Our shared fascination for southern Wisconsin, an interest that sometimes borders on obsession, is difficult to otherwise understand."

Through the special insights of modern-day seers, who have lent their higher vision to unraveling some of Wisconsin's prehistoric enigma, we have deepened our feeling for Rock Lake's mysterious past. But what of its future?

The Lake Threatened
Unfortunately, a prophet is not necessary to realize that the observers who have seen the underwater structures may be the last as well as the first such witnesses. From 1900, when they were spotted for the first time, until the mid-1930s, free divers were able to swim down to see and touch them with little effort. But beginning at the end of that decade, with the growth of the surrounding town of Lake Mills, pollutants and agricultural run-off were affecting the lake. Positive efforts at pollution control were made by local residents in the 1960s, and there can be no doubt that they largely rescued their beloved body of water from destruction. But the silt layer continued to increase, as subsurface visibility waned. Even during the eight years of our research at the lake, we have seen its underwater clarity go from bad to worse. The diving season of 1992 was unquestionably our worst, with visibility usually no more than three feet.

The front page report and photo in a December edition of the *Watertown Daily Times* told the sad story. It quoted Dave Marshall, Department of Natural Resources water biologist for Jefferson County, as saying, "High levels of phosphorous, nitrogen, and suspended solids are entering the lake from four or five construction sites in or near Shorewood Hills on the northwest side of the lake in the town of Lake Mills. All the sediment running into the lake will provide a habitat for more weed growth. It is providing nutrients for weeds and algae. There is no magic number, but the amount is considered high. Both are crucial nutrients for rooted aquatic plant growth."[2] At the present rate of construction run-off, the sunken monuments will be impossible to see after the turn of the next century.

It seems worse than ironic that the late twentieth century technology that allowed us to find the lost monuments of Rock Lake is simultaneously concealing them from future generations. It is a historical parallel we must appreciate, if our own civilization is to survive the coming one hundred years.

Casting her thoughts far beyond even this twenty-first century prospect, Lorraine Darr envisioned a time "when the lake will be no more. Where today it glistens as an enticing, intriguing body of spring-fed water teeming with bass and gar, a depressed marshland will spread like a bright green carpet of weeds and stubby growth. Hardly more than quaint curiosities, only the top, badly ruined and eroded portions of two or three of the smaller conical towers will protrude among the wildflowers. Originally the tombs of kings and astronomer-priests, their crumbling walls will be home to muskrats and tanagers. No one will suspect the existence of the inverted cone-shaped monuments, volcano-like sepulchers and colossal stone mound once venerated as the Temple of the Moon lying under the lightless ground. Forgotten will be all memory of the old city of the dead that so long ago went down under the waters of a vanished lake.

"The spirit-guardian will have long since disappeared forever into the deepest bowels of the planet, because the shrines left in his keeping will no longer require protection from the prying eyes of intruders. Finally at rest, the spirits of what used to be Rock Lake will sleep the undisturbed slumber of oblivion within the bosom of Mother Earth."

A Rock Lake Time Line

12,000 Years Before Present—

A retreating glacier carves out Rock Lake.

3000 B.C.—

Overseas metallurgists arrive at Michigan's Upper Peninsula to initiate copper mining on a massive scale. Rock Lake is almost simultaneously discovered by Atlantean prospectors from the Canary Island of Gran Canaria and named after their leading family, Tirajana, later remembered in native American tradition as Tyranena. It is established as a strategically located clearinghouse for mineral shipments to Bronze Age Europe. The first stone pyramids, temples, shrines, and tombs for the honored dead are built along the lake shore. Over the next eighteen centuries, the Wisconsin Tirajana grows to become a sacred center and necropolis.

1198 B.C.—

With the seismic destruction of Atlantis, the link between America's copper supplies and Europe's Bronze Age markets is broken. Michigan's mines close down and Tirajana is abandoned, but not before its necropolis is flooded by either an artificial deluge brought about by a canal opened to a nearby tributary of the Rock River; a pole shift that wrecks havoc with the whole planet; or some other natural explanation lost to history. During the following 1,700 years, Tyranena is continuously revered among the Plains Indians, although it is not resettled.

A.D. 900—

The Canari of Ecuador, descendants of the Atlantean Canari who settled in Wisconsin, institute copper as the Mesoamerican medium of exchange throughout Middle and South America. The Michigan mines reopen to provide mineral supplies for the new copper-based economy. Meanwhile, large contingents of Maya miners and astronomer-priests leave Yucatan, sailing north along the eastern shores of Mexico and up the Mississippi, finally establishing themselves in southwestern Illinois, across the river from the site of modern-day St. Louis. They build a megalopolis, Cahokia, which achieves phenomenal prosperity, as the capital of intercontinental copper trade.

A.D. 1100—

Astronomer-priests inform their people that the sacred calendar demands the abandonment of Cahokia. Seven families or tribes migrate to the Rock Lake area and build a similar though scaled-down version of their home town. They call it Chicomoztoc, or "Lake of the Seven Caves," or "Lake of the Womb." It is also known as an Aztalan, a "Water Town," because its eastern boundary faces a tributary of the Rock River, the Crawfish. As such, its generic name is remembered and passed down over the generations by Winnebago residing in the area. The "Beaded Princess" arrives in Aztalan with other Mayan aristocrats from the sister city of Tulum in distant Yucatan. The shores of Tyranena are used once more for burials. Over the next two centuries, the Aztalaners, now in control of the copper trade, achieve great wealth.

After A.D. 1300—

Some member of the Chicomoztoc (Aztalan) aristocracy marries an area native, who introduces a cannibalistic death-cult into the city, dividing society between adherents and opponents of the new religion. A severe drought ravages southern Wisconsin for several years, decimating crops and making fresh water scarce. Native copper deposits in Mexico are found, negating Aztalan's importance as a clearinghouse for the Michigan mines, which shut down.

A.D. **1320 to 1325—**
Reading their sacred calendar, the astronomer-priests order Chico-moztoc abandoned. The Aztalaners burn it to the ground to purify the desecrated sacred center, then migrate southward into the valley of Mexico. There, they build a new city, Tenochítlan, Place of the Stone Cactus, capital of the Aztec Empire, and modeled after their earlier residence in the far north. Two centuries later, after the Spanish conquistadors arrive in Mexico, the descendants from Aztalan are known as "Aztecs."

Early 19th century—
European settlers arriving in the Rock Lake area are told about the sunken "rock tepees" by local Winnebagos.

1900—
During an exceptional period of water clarity caused by a drought, two residents out on a small boat see one of the Rock Lake structures for the first time.

1937—
The earliest scuba exploration of Rock Lake locates a tall, stone pyramid shaped like an inverted ice-cream cone near the south end.

1989—
A sonar sweep of Rock Lake reveals several different manmade monuments on the bottom, including three effigy mounds.

1991—
The first useful underwater photographs of the Rock Lake structures are taken.

1991—
A stone pyramid is photographed twenty feet beneath the surface of Rock Lake atop a hill that was formerly an island.

Notes

Introduction: Magic on the Lake

1. John Robert Colombo, *Mysterious Canada: Strange Sights, Extraordinary Events and Peculiar Places* (Toronto: Doubleday Canada Ltd., 1989, 257, 258.

Chapter 2: Missing—Half a Billion Pounds of Copper

1. Octave DuTemple, ed. *Ancient Copper Mines of Upper Michigan* (Barrel, MI: Marlin Press, 1962, available through Michigan Public Library System's Inter-Library Loan), 12.
2. William P.F. Ferguson, "Michigan's Most Ancient Industry: The Pre-historic Mines and Miners of Isle Royale," in DuTemple, 54.
3. Roy W. Drier, "Prehistoric Mining in the Copper Country," in DuTemple, 73.
4. Ibid.
5. DuTemple, 12.
6. Jacob Houghton, "The Ancient Copper Miners of Lake Superior," in DuTemple, 80.
7. N.H. Winchell, "Ancient Copper Mines of Isle Royale," *The Engineering and Mining Journal* 32 (July to December 1881): 102.
8. Jacob Houghton, "The Ancient Copper Mines of Isle Royale," in DuTemple, 82.
9. George Brendt, "Great Lakes Geology," *North American Geological Symposium* (1983): 33.
10. William P. Scott, "Reminiscences of Isle Royale," *Michigan History Magazine* 9 (1933): 398.
11. *Encyclopaedia Britannica* (15th ed., London, 1981), *Micropaedia* II:1043.

12. S.A. Barrett, "Ancient Aztalan," *Bulletin of the Public Museum of the City of Milwaukee* 13 (1933): 56.

13. C. Harry Benedict, *Red Metal* (Ann Arbor: University of Michigan Press, 1958), 133.

14. Drier, 76.

15. George R. Fox, "The Ancient Copper Workings on Isle Royale" *The Wisconsin Archaeologist* 10 (1915): 74.

16. Ibid., 88.

17. Angus Murdoch, *Boom Copper* (New York: The MacMillan Company, 1943), 127.

18. Ibid., 202.

19. Drier, 77.

20. Dean James Savage, "Dug for Copper in Prehistoric Days," *Sunday Mining Gazette* (Calumet, Michigan), 7 May 1911).

21. Ferguson, 56.

22. Charles Whittlesey, "The Ancient Miners of Lake Superior," *Annals of Science* 1 (August 1852).

23. W.H. Holmes, "Aboriginal Copper Mines of Isle Royale, Lake Superior," *The American Anthropologist* 3 (1901), 684.

24. Samuel L. Smith, "Prehistoric and Modern Copper Mines of Lake Superior," *Michigan Historical Collections* 39 (1915), 137.

25. Edna Kenton, *The Indians of North America*, selected and edited from *The Jesuit Relations and Allied Documents* (New York: Harcourt, Brace and Company,1927), 123.

26. Ibid., 79.

27. Ibid., 88.

28. DuTemple, 14.

29. W. Pitezel, *Missionary Life* (Cincinnati: Walden and Stowe, 1857), 424.

30. Jack Parker, "The First Copper Miners," *Compressed Air Magazine,* January 1975, 8.

31. James Fisher, "Historical Sketch of the Lake Superior Copper District," *Mining Gazette* (Lansing: Michigan College of Mining and Technology), 7 September 1929.

32. Houghton, 81.

33. Betty Sodders, *Michigan Prehistory Mysteries* (AuTrain, Michigan: Avery Color Studios, 1991), 2:97.

34. Reuben G. Thwaites, *The Jesuit Relations and Allied Documents* (Cleveland: 1901), 4:24.
35. Sodders, 2:124.
36. Drier, 78.
37. Barrett, 173.
38. Charles E. Brown, *The Wisconsin Archaeologist* 5 (September 1926).
39. DuTemple, 21.
40. Jerry Ambelang, "Aztalan: U.S. Stonehenge?" *The Capital Times* (Madison, Wisconsin), 22 December 1986.
41. DuTemple, 18.
42. Whittlesey.
43. Parker, 11.
44. Ibid., 7.
45. Fox, 83.

Chapter 3: Atlantis and the Copper Question

1. Eberhard Zangerer, *The Flood from Heaven* (New York: William Morrow and Co., 1992), 126.
2. James Bailey, *The God-Kings and the Titans* (New York: St. Martin's Press, 1973), 110; Jurgen Spannmuth, *Atlantis of the North* (New York: Doubleday and Co., 1968), 173; Francis Joseph, *The Destruction of Atlantis* (Olympia Fields, Illinois: Atlantis Research Publishers, 1987), 64.
3. Plato, *Timaeus and Critias* (London: Penguin Books, 1977), 38.
4. Thucydides, *History of the Peloponnesian War* (New York: Randal Publishers,1922), 34.
5. Robert Ambrose, *Classical Greek and English Dictionary* (London: Rutherford Press, Ltd., 1959), 787.
6. Ignatius Donnelly, *Atlantis: The Antediluvian World* (New York: Harper's, 1882), 246.
7. Edward Herbert Thompson, *People of the Serpent* (New York: Capricorn Books, 1960), 16, 17.
8. Thwaites, 56.
9. George E. Langford, *Native American Legends* (New York: Doubleday and Company,1961), 121.
10. Paul Radin, *The Winnebago Tribe,* 37th Annual Report of the Bureau of American Ethnology, Smithsonian Institution, Washington, D.C., 1923. (Reprint. University of Nebraska Press, 1970), 110.

11. Ibid., 54, 55.

12. Vincent H. Gaddis, *Native American Myths and Mysteries* (California: Borderland Sciences, 1991), 48.

13. David H. Childress, *Lost Cities and Ancient Mysteries of South America* (Stelle, IL: Adventures Unlimited Press, 1986), 98.

14. Taylor L. Hansen, *The Ancient Atlantic* (Wisconsin: Amherst Press, 1969), 127.

15. Ibid., 129.

16. Salvador Lopez Herrera, *The Canary Islands Through History*, trans. Veronica de la Torre (Santa Cruz de Tenerife, Canary Islands: Graficas Tenerife, S.A., 1978), 40.

17. Campbell Grant, *The Rock Paintings of the Chumash* (Berkeley: University of California Press, 1966), 67.

18. Ibid., 64.

19. Ibid., 51.

20. Ibid.

21. Ibid.

22. Ibid., 60.

23. Anthony Mercatante, *Who's Who in Egyptian Mythology* (New York: Clarkson N. Potter, 1978), 75.

24. Plato, 139.

25. Spannuth, 114.

26. DuTemple, 18.

Chapter 4: Atlanteans Take Over America

1. Maitland A. Edey, *The Sea-Traders* (New York: Time-Life Books, 1974), 56.

2. Dorothy Hosler (with Heather Lechtman and Olaf Holm), "Axe-Monies and their Relatives," *Studies in Prehistoric Art and Archaeology* 30 (Washington, D.C.: Dumbarton Oaks Research Library and Collection, 1990).

3. Sodders, 86.

4. Ibid., page 102.

5. Ibid., page 98.

6. G.F. Kunz, *The Curious Lore of Precious Stones* (New York: Lippincott, 1913), 178.

7. Harold Buford, *Ancient Mexican Mythology* (New York: Ragnar Bros., 1955), 127.

8. Genesis 4:8.

9. Buford, 125.

10. Colin McEvedy, *The Penguin Atlas of Ancient History* (London: Penguin Books,1980), 33.

11. Zangerer, 125.

12. Zelia Nuttall, *Fundamental Principles of Old and New World Civilizations* (Cambridge: Peabody Museum, Harvard University, 1900), 2:197.

13. Glen Black, *Angel Site* (Indianapolis: University of Indiana Press, 1965), 2:86.

14. *National Archaeological Museum Catalog* 34:121 (Athens, Greece, 1968), 504.

15. Black, 103.

16. Hosler, 39.

17. Ibid., 93.

18. Ibid., 79.

19. Plato, 136, 137.

20. Arthur Colterell, *The MacMillan Illustrated Encyclopaedia of Myths and Legends* (New York: MacMillan, 1989), 68.

21. Sabas Martin, *Ritos y Leyendas Guanches* (Madrid: Miraguano Ediciones, 1988), 133.

22. J.E. Zimmerman, *Dictionary of Classical Mythology* (New York: Bantam Books, 1971), 98.

23. John Harms, *Romance and Truth in the Canary Islands* (Phoenix: Acorn Press,1965), 122.

24. Zimmerman, 58.

25. Robert MacNaughton, *Irish Myth* (New York: Scribners and Sons, 1924), 77.

26. Black, 103.

Chapter 5: The Rock Lake Mystery: A Worldwide Phenomenon

1. Gaddis, 36, 37.

2. Ibid.

3. Childress, 132.

4. Donnelly, 416.

5. Herbert Sawinski, letter to the author 9 May 1992.

6. John Wolford, "Stone Mounds of Oakland County," *The Ancient American* 1:3, (November 1993), 36.

7. Nobuhiro Yoshida of Kitakyushu-City, Japan, letter to the author 12 June 1992.

8. Childress, 133.

Chapter 6: What do the Stone Mounds Conceal?

1. James H. Kellar, "The C.L. Lewis Stone Mound and the Stone Mound Problem" (Ph.D. diss., publication 19,464, Ann Arbor: University Microfilms, 1956; and *Prehistory Regular Series* 3:4, Indianapolis: Indiana Historical Society, June 1960), 371.

2. Ibid., 383.

3. Ibid., 429.

4. Ibid., 368.

5. Ibid., 389.

6. Ibid., 393.

7. Glynn Daniel, *Encyclopaedia of Archaeology* (New York: Thomas Y. Crowell Co., 1977), 8, 9.

8. Kellar, 420.

9. Ibid., 422.

10. Ibid.

11. Ibid., 389.

12. Ibid., 446.

Chapter 7: New Revelations, New Enigmas

1. Brian Fagan, *New Treasures of the Past* (London: Quarto Publishers, 1987), 75.

2. Sodders, 151.

3. David H. Childress, *Lost Cities of North and Central America* (Stelle, IL: Adventures Unlimited Press,1992), 325.

4. Hans Schumacher, *World Myth* (New York: McHenry Publishers, 1954), 231.

5. James P. Valiga and Donna M. Stehling, "The Gottschall Site Rock Paintings," *The Journal of the Ancient Earthworks Society* 1 (1 January 1987), 138.

6. Paul Radin, *Winnebago Hero Cycles: A Study in Aboriginal Literature,* Indiana University Publications in Anthropology and Linguistics, (Baltimore: Waverly Press, 1948), 115–137.

7. Ibid.

8. Ibid.
9. Valiga and Stehling, 142.
10. Ibid., 147.
11. Ibid., 142.

Chapter 9: The Scuba Inventer and the Indian Teacher

1. Charles Berlitz, *Atlantis: The Eighth Continent* (New York: Fawcett Crest, 1984), 100.
2. Gaddis, 89.
3. Gunnar Thompson, *Nu Sun: Asian-American Voyages 500 B.C.* (California: Pioneer Press, 1989).

Chapter 10: Paranormal Occurrences

1. Fanny Davis, *The Palace of Topkapi in Istanbul* (New York: Charles Scribners & Sons, 1970), 3.
2. Frank Joseph, *The Lost Pyramids of Rock Lake* (St. Paul: Galde Press, 1992), 94.
3. Mary Wilson, *A History of Lake Mills* (Madison: Omnipress, 1983), 374.

Chapter 11: Psychics at the Sacred Center

1. Catherine C. Lorber, Number 130, Auction 30, Numismatic Fine Arts International, Inc., Los Angeles, California, 1992.
2. Elena Whishaw, *Atlantis in Andalusia* (New York: MacMillan, 1965).
3. Donald L. Lenzen, *Ancient Meteorology* (Tampa: Lenzen, 1989), 84, 85.
4. Plato, 137.

Chapter 12: The Psychics and the Artifacts

1. Edgar Cayce, *Edgar Cayce on Atlantis* (Virginia Beach: A.R.E. Publishers, 1968), 121.
2. Michael McManus, *Myths of the Irish People* (Chicago: Regnery, 1979), 64.
3. Lionel Casson, *Ships and Sailors of the Ancient World* (Maryland: Grensch Publishing Family, 1978), 99.
4. Barrett, 151.

Chapter 13: The Return of the Beaded Princess

1. Barrett, 163.
2. Bruce C. Hunter, *A Guide to Ancient Maya Ruins* (Norman: University of Oklahoma Press, 1977), 182.
3. R. Gordon Wasson, *The Wondrous Mushroom: Mycolatry in Mesoamerica* (New York: McGraw Hill Book Company, 1980), 148.
4. Alfonso Caso, *The Aztecs: People of the Sun* (Norman: University of Oklahoma Press, 1958), 74.

Chapter 14: A Psychic Overview of Rock Lake and Aztalan

1. Paul Gericke, *History of Lake Mills* (Lake Mills, Wisconsin: 13 February 1936), 66.
2. Margaret Krueger, "Erosion Promotes Growth of Rock Lake Weed Areas," *Watertown* (Wisconsin) *Daily Times*, 31 December 1992, 1.

THE LOST PYRAMIDS OF ROCK LAKE
by Frank Joseph

Was Atlantis in Wisconsin? Now, for the first time, here is proof of ancient, sacred pyramids at the bottom of a small lake in Wisconsin! Learn about the fascinating secrets of a great people who erected structures on land and in water as sophisticated astronomical observatories for their bloody sky cult.

This lake is forty miles west of Milwaukee, Wisconsin. In 1989 author Frank Joseph organized the first side-scan sonar sweep of Rock Lake for the elusive structures. His instruments revealed an unprecedented panorama on the lake floor by way of images transposed from sound waves. The high-tech method identified a colossal stone mound shaped like an elongated pyramid sixty feet below the surface, and his research subsequently received widespread attention in the regional press.

Joseph has traveled the world over for revealing clues to the lost history of prehistoric Wisconsin, and is presently working with state authorities to have Rock Lake declared an official historic site. Trace the development of this ancient culture and read about amazing parallels with similar prehistoric cultures in the Canary Islands.

1-880090-04-X, 6 x 9, 212 pages
illustrated, softcover
$10.95

To order *The Lost Pyramids of Rock Lake* or additional copies of *Atlantis in Wisconsin,* please send price of book(s) plus $2.00 postage and handling for the first book and 50¢ for each additional book to:

Galde Press, Inc.
PO Box 65611
St. Paul, Minnesota 55165
(612) 891-5991
Fax (612) 891-6091
For orders call 1-800-777-3454